ALL ABOUT ROAD RACING

by
tom heinonen &
janet heinonen

First published in 1979 by Tafnews Press,
Book Division of Track & Field News,
Box 296, Los Altos, California 94022 USA.

Library of Congress Catalog Card Number 78-68730
Standard Book Number 0-911520-91-0

Printed in the United States of America

Cover Design: Ann Andrew
Layout: Suzie Carlyon
Production Assistants: Grace Light, Debbie Sims

PHOTO CREDITS

6	Tim Carlson/WGBH-TV
22	Steve Murdock
27	WGBH-TV
29	Jeff Johnson
30	Long Photography, Inc.
40	Jim Engle
46	Rick Levy
79	Warren Morgan
90	Ruth Laney
98	Warren Morgan
106	Warren Morgan
110-112	Warren Morgan
118	Warren Morgan

TABLE OF CONTENTS

ABOUT THE AUTHORS 4

CHAPTER 1: THE HISTORY OF ROAD RACING 7

CHAPTER 2: SELECTING RACES 31

CHAPTER 3: TRAINING FOR ROAD RACES 47

CHAPTER 4: RACING 77

CHAPTER 5: INJURIES 97

CHAPTER 6: AUXILIARY AIDS FOR RUNNERS . . . 107

APPENDIX 122

PREFACE

This book is written for all men and women who enjoy competitive distance running. We do not intend to be sexist but we have used the conventional masculine form of the pronoun rather than deal with the sticky "he/she" or "(s)he" form of the pronoun which have limited practical use. When we refer to the runner as "he," we are referring to runners of both sexes unless stated otherwise.

ABOUT THE AUTHORS

Between them, Tom and Janet Heinonen have a wide and varied background in running which includes a combined 27 years of road racing and 39 years of competitive running on four continents.

Tom, 33, was one of the leading marathoners in the United States in the late 1960s after a distinguished running career at the University of Minnesota. He was the Big Ten three-mile champion in 1967 and placed third in the NCAA six-mile the same year, having also been an NCAA scorer in 1965 and 1966. After graduation from Minnesota in 1968, Heinonen became more active on the road racing scene, winning the 1969 AAU Marathon and the 1975 Trail's End Marathon. He has a best of 2:18:30 for the marathon and remains an active road racer.

Heinonen made five international trips to Europe and Africa in cross country and coached distance runners as a Peace Corps volunteer in Chile. He earned a Master's degree in Physical Education at the University of Oregon in 1975 and has coached the Oregon women's cross country team since 1975. His teams have placed seventh or better at AIAW cross country

4

nationals every year. He was named head women's track coach at Oregon in 1976. Heinonen has attended two national training camps for elite women distance runners and coaches, at the invitation of the U.S. Olympic Committee. He was also involved in high altitude research in 1967 and 1968, prior to the Mexico City Olympics.

Heinonen has been an active member of the Twin Cities Track Club, San Diego Track Club and the Oregon Track Club. He and his wife, Janet, sponsor monthly fun runs in their hometown of Eugene, Oregon.

Janet, 27, began her running as a grade school disciple of Bill Bowerman's jogging program. She moved into competitive track, cross country and road racing in high school and was a pioneer in women's road racing, competing in her first marathon in 1970. While making no claims at being a national class talent, Janet "keeps improving" each year and considers a 10:58 two-mile and a 2:06 30-kilometer her best marks.

Janet has been a long-time track fan, raised on the excitement surrounding Hayward Field in Eugene, site of numerous national track championships. She has been an active force in promoting women's running in her area, having organized a women's 24-hour relay team, lobbied for women's events in track meets and a combined men's and women's Olympic Trials and directed several national class road and track distance races for women. She also organizes competition for Oregon Track Club women and served as editor of the club's newsletter for three years.

She graduated from the University of Oregon in 1972 and served briefly in the Peace Corps where she coached Dora Gonzalez, the first South American woman to run the marathon, and introduced women to road racing. She returned to Oregon to complete work on a Master's degree in journalism. In 1976 she was hired to a regular staff position at Oregon as women's S.I.D. Janet has been a free-lance contributor to Runner's World since 1969 and has recently completed another book on running, *Sports Illustrated Running for Women.*

1
THE HISTORY OF ROAD RACING

"The entire continent is suffering an epidemic of Marathonitis in its most violent form. One cannot stroll in any big pleasure ground between Central Park, N.Y., and Golden Gate Park, in San Francisco, without seeing scores of youths, head up and elbows in, plodding along at the regular monotonous jog trot which tells that they are training for the classic course of 26 miles, 385 yards. The country roads are full of candidates in the throes of preparation. No athletic meeting is complete without the marathon event."

A recent issue of *The New Yorker?* Hardly. Those comments appeared in *Harper's Weekly* in 1909.

FOOT RACING CRAZE NOT A NEW PHENOMENON

Although the 1970s have brought to the United States the biggest boom in competitive running the country has ever known, the phenomenon itself is not new—it's just emerging from hibernation.

Foot racing is one of the oldest of sports, with the Greeks being among the first to formalize it in the Ancient Olympic Games. The development of foot racing in modern times has been noted sporadically throughout the pages of history. In 1660 Pepys recorded foot-racing in London's Hyde Park and a purse of 1,000 pounds for a one mile race in Woodstock, Oxfordshire. In 1801, *Sporting Magazine* noted that a 15-year-old English girl ran a mile in 5:28 in 1795 to win a two-guinea wager.

Modern track and field and foot racing gained steam in the 19th century. The British held distance races for cash prizes in 1825 about the time amateur events also began to flourish. The first organized track meet of modern times was promoted by the Royal Military Academy in 1849.

During the 1830s, long distance races were either amateur races, such as the Crick Run (11 1/8 miles) at Rugby School in England in 1837, or professional events with large purses.

Professional distance races spread to the United States during the 1830s as well. One of the noted races of the time came in 1835 at Union Course on Long Island. A $1,000 purse was offered for the ten mile race with a special prize to be awarded for bettering an hour. Henry Stannard won the race and the bonus, running the distance in 59.44.

By the mid-1840s, these ten-mile races were quite popular in the States, drawing huge crowds. An internationally-flavored race in 1844 drew 25,000 spectators to Beacon Course in Hoboken, N.J. to watch England's Thomas Greenhalgh and John Barlow take on top American runners. John Gildersleeve, A New York chair guilder, won the race in 57:01, collecting $700 while Greenhalgh and Barlow took second and third, respectively. An 1845 engraving of the Hoboken race shows the racers in knee pants, some shirtless, one with suspenders. An enthusiastic crowd flowed onto the course, crushing in on the racers.

Barlow, the Englishman, clocked a speedy 54:21 in another ten-miler, defeating John Steeprock, an American Indian, as well as Gildersleeve. These professional runners, known as pedestrians or "peds" were popular on both sides of

8

the Atlantic from 1830 to 1860.

One of the top peds of the 1840s was William Jackson, known as the "American Deer." Jackson, like his competitors, wore his own colors when he raced, as jockeys do today. Pat Mahoney, a running butcher, wore a green shirt, blue breeches and white stockings. George Crammer, a running carpenter, had a suit of white silk with a red belt and pink slippers. One of the all-time running greats, a Seneca Indian named Deerfoot, took theatrical advantage of his background and wore a breechcloth, moccasins and a feather. In 1861 Deerfoot traveled to England to compete in races which attracted members of the royal family. He preferred to race at distances ten miles and longer and was a consistent winner.

Race walking became more prominent in the 1870s and 1880s, along with "go-as-you-please" races which generally lasted several days with competitors walking or running, as they pleased.

Edward Weston was one of the big names in walking, starting in 1861 when, at the age of 22, he walked from Boston to Washington (478 miles) in ten days—on a bet—to see Lincoln inaugurated. A half century later, Weston walked from New York to San Francisco in 105 days to celebrate his 70th birthday. Weston also competed in one of the better known events of the day, the Astley Belt Competition in Gilmore's Garden, the forerunner of the Madison Square Garden.

In 1878 Sir John Astley, a member of Parliament, offered 500 pounds to the winner of a six-day, go-as-you-please race. Daniel O'Leary won the race, beating runner-up John Hughes, 403 miles to 310, giving rise to challenges and ensuing races. In 1879 Weston, who held the six-day record of 530 miles, lined up against 12 contestants in the Garden. Weston was unable to match his record and ended up fifth as Charles Powell of England won the race, approximating Weston's mark. The record was later improved to 623 miles in six days according to one source.

Following the Civil War, the amateur movement gained momentum in the United States with the founding of the New York Athletic Club ((NYAC) in 1868. Other amateur clubs developed in large cities and professional foot racing eventually became a thing of the past.

The NYAC held the first indoor track meet in the U.S. in 1868 and in 1876 the first national amateur championships were held, as well as the first collegiate championships in the U.S. (the IC4A). The English experienced a similar growth in amateur athletics with a national organization being founded in 1866 and 40 amateur clubs in existence by 1880.

The National Amateur Athletic Union (AAU) in the U.S. was formed in 1879, and by 1887 American records had progressed to the following: 100 yards (10.0), 220 (22.0), 440 (47¾), 880 (1:55 2/5), mile (4:21 2/5), ten-mile (52:58 3/5). Most track meets during the late 1880s also scheduled five-mile races.

While track races were gaining official sanction, foot racing was taking a more informal, recreational turn, called the paper chase or "Hare and Hounds." Paper chases were introduced in the United States in 1874; Harvard was the first American college to take up the sport, in 1881. Paper chases were races run over rough terrain, covering some five to twelve miles with one person (the hare) setting the trail with paper while the rest of the runners (the hounds) followed in pursuit. Perhaps it was inevitable that the paper chases developed into cross country races. "Hare-and-hounds and cross country runs are very popular just now among college men," noted *Outing* magazine in 1889.

Cross country races were sponsored by clubs as well as colleges. In January of 1889 the Prospect Harriers held a moonlight run of six miles in Brooklyn's Washington Park.

EARLY TRAINING METHODS

The sport of distance running must have reached a creditable state around the 1890s since training methods came under discussion. At that time paper chasing was regarded as a form of exercise or preliminary training for distance runners. Intercollegiate cross country competition started with a race between Pennsylvania and Cornell in 1890 and by 1898 there was a cross country boom in universities.

ALL ABOUT ROAD RACING

In an 1891 issue of *Outing*, Malcom Ford wrote about distance running:

"Novices often ask the question, 'How can I practice my distance, when every time I run it exhausts me so much that I do not feel like running again for many days?"

Ford exhorted the runner to differentiate between "lassitude and a genuine fatigue."

He also advised the runner, "preparatory to a seige at training for distance running," to take a purgative. He gave more germane advice when he remarked that most famous distance runners began by "taking sociable cross-country jogs with their friends."

W.G. George of England was a famous amateur runner who trained by following hounds across the country for ten or 15 miles. He ran because he enjoyed it and gave no thought to racing. He had been taking these jaunts for three or four years before competing. He ran a 4:18.4 mile as an amateur and then 4:12.7 as a professional.

MODERN AND ANCIENT OLYMPIC MARATHONS

Just as the modern Olympics spurred interest in track and field in general, so too they created a race which many regard as the epitome of Olympic athletics. Epitome or not, the legends and facts which surround the Olympic marathon have done much to make the marathon the glamour event of road racing, the event which quadriennially brings the world's respect to our sport.

The story of Pierre de Coubertin's Olympic dream, realized first in 1896 in Athens, is well known. Baron de Coubertin, a Frenchman whose prime interest was public education, firmly believed that mental and physical development were inseparable, a belief that was contrary to French tradition.

At the age of 26, in 1888, de Coubertin helped organize l'Union des Sports Athletiques to stimulate interest in physical education in his country. In 1889 he founded a monthly paper, *La Revue Athletique*, to spur interest in sport in France.

De Coubertin's interest took an international turn when he

travelled through Europe and North America to study physical education programs in various countries. His travels took him to the ruins at Olympia which had been excavated between 1875 and 1881.

Disturbed by the growing commercialism of international sport, de Coubertin dreamed up a cure, namely the revival of the ancient Greek Olympic Games.

After several years of lobbying for the idea, the Baron summoned an international athletic congress to join l'Union des Sports Athletiques at the Sorbonne in 1894. Delegates from nine countries attended the meeting, ostensibly to discuss only general topics of international athletics.

"I carefully refrained from mentioning such an ambitious project," said the Baron, "afraid it might raise such a storm of contempt and scorn as to discourage beforehand those who favored it."

De Coubertin sprung his plan upon the delegates. Stressing international understanding and youth fitness, he convinced even the most skeptical delegates. His proposal was to stage the first modern Olympic Games in Paris in 1900, as part of the city's International Exposition. But arguments from the Greek delegation and the precedents of the Greek's ancient Olympics convinced the congress to switch the site to Athens in 1896, with the Baron's approval.

The man who conceived the idea of including the "marathon" race in the modern Olympics was Michel Breal, a French writer and student of Greek mythology, who was a friend of de Coubertin's.

Breal wanted to commemorate the run of the legendary young Greek, Pheidippides. In 490 B.C. Pheidippides, a champion Olympic runner, was called upon by his Athenian general, Miltiades, to carry news of a stunning military victory from the plains of Marathon to the market place in Athens. Already weary from a day of battle, the runner set off on his mission, running some twenty-five miles to Athens. "Rejoice—we conquer!" he cried to the Athenians, then collapsed and died.

The whole legend of Pheidippides has come under scrutiny

by modern historians, and perhaps marathon runners of this century should be thankful that the legend of Pheidippides differed greatly from the actual information which historians have recorded through the years about the distance runner.

Reference books give differing accounts of the famous runner. Several of them mention that he had run to Sparta and back to ask for help against the Persian invaders. On his return to the plain of Marathon he had only enough time to join in the battle before taking off on his more famous run to Athens. Unfortunately, no historians of that time so much as mentioned the run from Marathon to Athens although Pheidippides was given credit by Herodotus, the father of history, with running from Athens to Sparta and back (some 228 kilometers) in two days, carrying the request for help.

With one exception, the Marathon story of 490 B.C. remained unknown for centuries. Plutarch (46 to 120 A.D.) mentioned a story about a runner named Euchidas who supposedly ran from the battle field at Plataea to Delphi in 479 B.C. and back, a distance of some 200 kilometers, to fetch the Holy Fire for purification rites. Upon greeting his fellow citizens and handing them the Holy Fire, wrote Plutarch, he fell down and died. His gravestone carried the following inscription: "Having run to Pythos (i.e. Delphi) Euchidas returned on the same day."

The first mention of the Pheidippides marathon story came shortly after Plutarch's death when Lucian (120 to 180 A.D.), a philosopher, satirist and fiction writer, wrote a short essay and mentioned Pheidippides' message of victory from Marathon and his subsequent death. Similarities in style and content with the stories of Herodotus and Plutarch lead modern historians to conclude that Lucian conveniently combined the stories to get a more effective example.

Lucian's version stayed alive through the centuries and achieved wide recognition through 19th century art. In 1834, the French sculptor Cortot created a statue of Pheidippides, Le Soldat de Marathon. Pheidippides stands in the garden of Tuilleries in Paris, reminding thousands of visitors of his story.

Fortunately for the 25 men lined up at the start of the

first modern Olympic Marathon on April 10, 1896, the distance ahead of them was closer to 40 kilometers, rather than the 200 kilometers which might be more accurately associated with the history of the race.

A Greek colonel named Papadiamantopolous fired his revolver to start the race, sending the runners on their way to Athens with horse-drawn carts bearing doctors and medical supplies following at a discreet distance. The Colonel had a special interest in the race, namely a Greek shepherd, Spiridon Loues, who had served under the Colonel in the Greek First Infantry Regiment, and had demonstrated great endurance and stamina during long marches. The Colonel, a member of the organizing committee for the Olympics, urged Loues to enter.

The Greeks felt a special poetic interest in the marathon race; what could be more fitting than for a Greek to win the race? Special efforts were made to develop distance men and in the winter of 1895-96 runners trained between the plain of Marathon and the capital city. Should the winner of the marathon race be a Greek, Athenian businessmen guaranteed that he be taken care of for life. They offered cash prizes, annuities, free restaurant meals for life; tailors, hotel keepers, barbers and hatters all made similar offers.

Among the top runners were the first three finishers in the 1500 meters—the Australian Edwin Flack, the American Arthur Blake and the Frenchman Albin Lermusiaux who told the press that his specialties were actually the 100 meter dash and the marathon. How did he train for such diverse events?

"One day I run a leetle way, vairy queek. Ze next day, I run a long way, vairy slow," he replied.

Why did he wear white gloves when he ran?

"Ah-ha! Zat is because I run for ze king!"

The irrepressible Frenchman took the early lead in the marathon, leading Flack by more than a mile after 30 minutes. Then came Blake, then a Hungarian, Gyula Kellner. Loues was back another few minutes. When worried villagers told the shepherd that he was far back from the leaders, he shrugged and said, "Never mind, I will overtake and beat them all."

Lermusieux still had the lead at 15 kilometers, then started

14   *ALL ABOUT ROAD RACING*

to fade badly. He was later accused of repeately sipping from a flask of brandy during the race. Flack took over the lead while Blake, a miler by habit, was forced by exhaustion to quit at 23 kilometers. An uphill grade slowed Lermusiaus to a walk. Soon after, Flack passed him, and the Greek shepherd took command of second place.

Lermusiaux dropped out at 32 kilometers, completely spent. At 33 kilometers Loues took the lead with Flack staying at close range, some 20 meters back.

Flack, who only the day before had added a gold medal in the 800 meters to his gold for the 1500, began to falter at 36 kilometers and Loues sprinted farther ahead as the Australian collapsed.

An ecstatic Greek crowd of 70,000 cheered on the shepherd from Maroussi as he entered the stadium, obviously weary, but still holding good form. Greek Prince George and Crown Price Constantine left the royal party to run beside Spiridon Loues on his final lap. Seven minutes ahead of his nearest competitor, Loues completed the 40 kilometer run in 2:58:50 and all Greece rejoiced. To add to their joy, five of the first six finishers in the race were also Greeks.

THE BOSTON MARATHON

The Boston Athletic Association (B.A.A.) had sent a large delegation to the Olympic Games in Athens where the marathon had stirred so much interest. The B.A.A. decided to stage its own marathon in the United States but New York beat the B.A.A. to the starting line.

The first marathon run in the United States started in Stamford, Conn. and finished in Columbus Circle, New York City, a distance of approximately 25 miles. New Yorker J.J. McDermott was the winner of that first marathon in October of 1896.

Despite New York's headstart, the B.A.A. continued with its plans to sponsor a marathon, choosing April 19, 1897 as the inaugural date for the event, to commemorate Paul Revere's famous ride. The race would start in Ashland, at Metcalfe's Mill, and finish 24.7 miles later at the Irvington Street Oval in Boston, in conjunction with a track meet.

A field of 15 runners, including six from New York, started the race. The runners set off down the course and dusty roads, well-attended by militiamen and bicycling ambulance corpsmen who flanked the runners. McDermott, who was the favorite after his New York victory, emerged as the leader. No one was close enough to press him as he slowed in the final miles, stopping to walk three times from Boston College (at 22 miles) to the finish. Coming on to Massachusetts Avenue, near the finish, McDermott ran smack into a funeral procession, causing two electric cars to stall.

Undaunted, the slight runner continued on to the Irvington Street Oval, completing the course in 2:55:10, some seven minutes ahead of the next runner, James Kiernan. McDermott lost ten pounds during the race, going from 124 to 114.

Since that inauspicious start in 1897, The Boston Marathon has grown to be the most famous international road race, rivalled only by the quadriennial Olympic Marathon. In 1909, at the height of the marathon craze, Boston had 164 entrants.

MARATHON MADNESS

At the time when marathon madness was starting to reach its zenith in the United States, writer William Hemmingway looked back upon the phenomenon, saying that it all started in Hamilton, Ontario, with a race that pre-dated the more famous Boston Marathon.

Hemmingway related the story of the Hamilton race in a 1909 issue of *Harper's Weekly,* and the story of this one race may reflect the beginnings of similar races across the continent, races dictated by geographical settings and a challenge.

During the Canadian winter Hamilton sportsmen got in the habit of walking around the local bay, a distance of 19 miles, 186 yards. The walk developed into something of a race with the fastest completing the course in four hours.

R.B. Harris, one of the owners of the Hamilton *Herald* newspaper, walked the distance in three hours and soon found his record challenged by others. He decided to offer a cup, sponsored by his newspaper, for a go-as-you-please race around the bay. In 1894, 12 men raced through snow and slush with W.R. Marshall playing tortoise and hare to win the race, running along at a 6:00 mile clip, then stopping to rest. He completed the distance in two-and-a-half hours. The next year the race was held in 90 degree heat on Labor Day and in 1896 the date was changed to early November, becoming an annual event. By 1909 the top runners were covering the distance in 1:55:00 and Hamilton had even produced the Olympic marathon champion in the so-called unofficial Olympics held in Athens in 1906. William Sherring of the Hamilton Shamrock Athletic Club was first to complete the famous Marathon to Athens course that year, in 2:51:23.6.

Road races continued in popularity until the shadows of World War I fell across Europe and North America. Young men, who devoted themselves to such pastimes as training for the Olympic marathon or racing in local contests associated with local athletic clubs or community festivals, now had to concern themselves with becoming soldiers.

TRUE CROSS-COUNTRY RACING: THE BUNION DERBY

Following World War I, long distance racing took a transcontinental turn. While more staid forms of road-racing, such as AAU sanctioned national championships and the traditional races of the New England area, were drawing runners, races crossing the United States were drawing publicity.

In 1928 *Outlook* magazine followed the course of what it termed "the most peculiar sporting event to be found in this country's history," a race from Los Angeles to New York.

Some 250 runners left Los Angeles but more than half dropped out before leaving California. The remaining runners were lured by the promise of $48,500 in prizes. The man behind the race was C.C. Pyle, fondly referred to as "Cold Cash" or "Corn and Callus" Pyle. The promoter hoped to collect from various towns en route to New York, by the "old means of bleeding the chambers of commerce with promises of nation-wide publicity."

Outlook reported that the field at the start was "as conglomerated a mass of human beings as ever entered any event of the sort in this country or perhaps the world." The race was expected to take 54 days with the favorite being Hannes Kolehmainen, the Finn who won the 1920 Olympic Marathon as well as the Olympic 5000 and 10,000 in 1912.

By six days out (207 miles) the field had dwindled considerably. Although the magazine reported only "30 to 50" runners left after six days, a subsequent issue counted 55 men running in Madison Square Garden in the closing scenes of the "Bunion Derby", 84 days out of Los Angeles.

"Three thousand looked on, apathetic in the main, even when Mr. "Wildfire" Thompson, one of the contestants, ran backwards."

The Finnish runner had dropped out in the early stages of the race and the eventual winner was Andrew Payne, a young Oklahoma Indian. His prize was to have been $25,000, "if Mr. C.C. Pyle is solvent and a man of his word."

Second place and $10,000 went to Johnny Salo of Passaic, N.J., $5,000 to third placer Philip Granville, a "towering Negro from Canada," and $2,500 to Mike Joyce, a Cleveland bartender-out-of-work, who finished fourth. One thousand dollars each went to Guisto Omek (Trieste, Italy), William Kerry (Minneapolis), Louis Perella (Albany), Ed Gardiner (Seattle), Fran von Flue (Kermac, California), and John Cronick (Saskatoon, Canada).

C.C. Pyle insisted vehemently that the winner would be paid, although, noted the magazine, "delivery was postponed a week, pending a special 24-hour relay race in the Garden."

It's doubtful if Payne, who completed the 3,422.2 miles in 573 hours, four minutes and 34 seconds running time, ever got his money. A summary of the event in a 1928 issue of *Literary Digest* pictured Payne standing in knee-length baggy white running shorts next to his "Paw," with the caption proclaiming that Payne, the Oklahoma farm boy, intended to lift the "inevitable mortgage" from his father's farm with his winnings.

However, C.C. Pyle himself was quoted as admitting at the end that the "red ink of a deficit adorned the ledgers of this particular project." Pyle, the impresario who also packaged and promoted tennis star Suzanne Lengler and football hero Red Grange, insisted that the best was yet to come: "I will not have to wait for the profits to accrue from the miraculous foot fixer (another Pyle scheme involving C.C. Pyle's Patent Foot Box, containing remedies 'for every one of the 3,000 maladies of the human foot') in order to pay my athletes their prizes . . . I will race the ten winners that I have under contract in marathons and twenty-six hour races in all the big cities of the country and hold bigger annual transcontinental derbies every year."

Others were less enthusiastic about the prospect of such events, terming the Bunion Derby "the flop of the century" (New York *Sun*). The *Evening News* described the race survivors as "emaciated scarecrows, unshaven, unshorn caricatures" in a "picture of commercialized sport in a form unedifying, to say the least."

The N.Y. Herald Tribune ridiculed the race, calling it an "Aching Dog Caravan." And indeed, C.C. Pyle, who reportedly sank $150,000 to $200,000 into the race, may have felt like an aching dog himself when all was done and funds from the towns along the route never materialized. After all, pointed out *Literary Digest*, how many people were interested in looking at a mass of blistered and exhausted bodies after the completion of the day's run?

BETWEEN WARS, THE FLYING FINNS

The marathon madness which gripped the country prior to the first World War was on the wane following the war. And the Olympic Marathon, the most prestigious road race in the world, was providing the United States with few long distance heroes. With the exception of Clarence DeMar's third place finish in the 1924 Games, no American won a medal in a post-World War I Olympic Marathon until Frank Shorter's win in Montreal in 1972.

Indeed, the distance races became the property of the

Finns. In the five Games held from 1920 to 1936 the Finns won an incredible 23 of 45 possible medals in the 5000, 10,000 and marathon. (They also accounted for eight of 15 medals in the steeplechase during that period.) The golden names of distance running were Paavo Nurmi, Ville Ritola and Albin Stenroos, all Finns, all Olympic gold medalists.

Although the sport of road racing was providing few top-flight Olympians during this period, moves in both England and the United States helped to establish and standardize the sport as we know it today. The marathon finally became official at the 26 mile, 385 yard distance and national championships were offered on the roads at varying distances (usually 15 to 30 kilometers or 10 to 20 miles).

Road racing hit a low during World War II when most of the runners and officials were involved in the war. Travel was restricted during that period and some long-time races had to be suspended.

ROAD RUNNERS CLUB SPURS INTEREST

Following World War II, road racing gradually came to life again. Races drew more participants and in various sections of the country local AAU organizations were quite active in promoting races through the Long Distance Running Committee. New England remained the hotbed of racing but the sport was also finding a following in the mid-Atlantic states where cross country races were the staple fare.

The runners frequenting these races were virtually all men, most of them out of school. (The AAU did not allow women to compete in distance races.) Some were track men turned road racers, others were strictly road racers and still others joined in the competition but admittedly trained little and were not very fit. The joggers and recreational racers of the 1960s and 1970s were an unknown breed at that time.

When it came time to race marathons, the true road runner counted on the track runner to crack up somewhere between 18 and 23 miles and start walking, recalls veteran distanceman Ted Corbitt.

20

Corbitt and fellow runner Browning Ross were two of the men who helped elevate the sport of road racing to the status it enjoys today, through the organization of the Road Runners Club of America.

The Road Runners Club started in England, under the direction of Ernest Neville who had been associated with the 52.5 mile London-to-Brighton walking races since the turn of the century. He conceived the RRC of England in 1952 to promote this ultra-marathon as an annual running event and to encourage all forms of long distance running. In a few years the number of road races in Britain tripled and the caliber of British long distance running increased phenomenally.

Ross, a runner with impressive road and track credentials (including eight national AAU titles), transplanted the idea to the U.S. after joining the English RRC while competing overseas.

Although he was also the National AAU Long Distance Chairman and editor of the first world-wide long distance running journal, *Long Distance Log,* Ross had trouble convincing American runners that a Road Runners Club would be to their benefit. Runners were suspicious of the idea and refused to join. They distrusted organizations and, since the 1880s, had been complaining bitterly that road running was always pushed aside by officials in favor of the more glamorous and profitable track races.

Ted Corbitt gave Ross his support, though, and agreed to become president of the club, a step which caused other runners to reconsider their position and give their support to the fledgling group. Corbitt requested sanction from the AAU but was turned down. "The AAU resisted the Road Runners Club in some areas. The AAU had controlled road racing by tradition and law and they saw our club as another possible headache," said Corbitt.

The RRC went ahead with its plans and sponsored its first race, a six-mile handicap, in September of 1958. As other races sprang up under the successful promotion of the RRC, the AAU changed its stand, realizing that the club was not out to challenge the AAU but rather to support a long-neglected arm of the group.

TED CORBITT, FATHER OF AMERICAN ULTRA-DISTANCE RUNNING.

ALL ABOUT ROAD RACING

Road racers had a close-knit fraternity during the early days of the Road Runners Club. "We were quite a mixture—the old-timers, high school kids, older runners, a few top runners," remembers Ross. "Everyone knew everyone else and the American Olympians (in the marathon) were all road racers."

Road runners were hardly the glamour boys of the American sports scene at that time, except at a few prestigious events such as the Boston Marathon and the Olympic Marathon. College track men snickered at road racers and the public cast a disapproving or bemused eye upon those skinny men in underwear who trotted through the streets.

"I felt sheepish when I trained. Kind of foolish. So I trained in the woods or on the track," said Ross.

Feeling foolish or not, Ross and his Road Runners Club and *Long Distance Log* gave a sense of unity to road racers and provided them with the impetus to promote races in their own areas. Races experienced a steady growth through the late 1950s and early 1960s. Some were put on solely by individuals; others were tied to local events, such as community festivals. Others were simply modern versions of races which started as bets, or which were thought up over more than a few beers in local drinking clubs.

With the introduction of jogging to the United States in the early 1960s, road runs began to experience a slight swelling in the ranks by people—men and women—who made a natural progression from jogging to fitness to low-key competitive running. Road racers began to achieve a new status. Those lean runners were obviously and enviably fitter and faster than the sedentary individual who recently had taken up jogging and was now trying his first road race.

The road racing ranks were also being bolstered by big-name track runners who were filtering into the roads. Most long distance track men were not yet at their physical peak when they finished their college careers and road racing, and marathoning was a logical extension of their competitive careers. No longer was it the true road racer who made the U.S. Olympic marathon team. Not since 1960 has the U.S. marathon contingent at the Olympics been composed of runners with little or no track background. By the late 1960s road races and marathons often were won by people like Bill Clark, Eamon O'Reilly and Ken Moore, all runners with impressive track credentials.

THE CURRENT ROAD RACING EXPLOSION

The ballooning interest in road races in the late 1970s is attributable to a running boom, not a racing boom. While most entrants in road races consider themselves "runners" (as opposed to "joggers"), few consider themselves "racers."

Although each year an increasing number of racers graduate from the ranks of runners, the exponential increase in race entrants is at the back of the pack, not the front.

Fitness runs, fun runs and family runs have offered the beginning runner a chance for low-key competition for well over a decade. Traditional road races such as those that have flourished for years in New England, have offered the more experienced runner a chance for more intense competition.

With a big push from commercial sponsors and other commercial interests (i.e., running shoes manufacturers), races have become events staged to lure all shapes and kinds of runners. Running with Frank Shorter or Bill Rodgers has become as much an event as running with the bulls in Pamplona.

How long the nouveau fit or the running chic will stay with us is open to debate. But it seems apparent that whatever their original motivations were for running, many who have discovered running will stick with it and of those sticking with the sport an increasing number will become racers—men and women who enjoy both the feeling of true fitness and the challenge of competition.

HISTORY OF WOMEN'S ROAD RACING

The ancient Greeks banned women, on penalty of death, from even viewing the Olympic Games. The Amateur Athletic Union of the United States banned a high school girl from competition for life because she ran in a marathon in the late 1950s.

While men's distance running experienced a predictable cycle of respectability, chicanery, exhibitionism and benign neglect, women's distance running experienced a vacuum.

It's not uncharacteristic of the women's side of the sport that the 5:28 mile run by the 15-year-old English girl in 1795 stood for 172 years as a world age group record.

Little happened in the hundred years following the English girl's run. Finland and Germany occasionally included a distance race for women in minor track meets in the early 1900s. France instituted an official 1000 meter championship for women in 1918 but the event wasn't even timed. The Soviet Union held 1000 and 1500 meter championships for women starting in 1922. In 1928 the women's 800 was included in the Olympic program for women. The Amsterdam race was a close one, with Germany's Lina Radke first in 2:16.8 and Japan's Kinuye Hitoma and Sweden's Inga Gentzel close behind in 2:17.6 and 2:17.8.

Unfortunately not all of the runners were fit enough to finish the race in good shape, as most of them were sprinters trying to find out whether they could finish 800 meters. After watching the finish, Olympic officials decreed that women should not run anything longer than 200 meters, a decision which stood for 32 years. It wasn't until Rome in 1960 that women were allowed to run the 400 and 800 meters. The 1500 wasn't added until 1972 and that still remains as the longest Olympic distance for women, even though men compete in three distance races longer than 1500 meters on the track as well as the marathon on the roads. Nonetheless, the top women in the world are quickly approaching marks which won Olympic medals for Finns like Nurmi, Ritola and Stenroos. And this despite the fact that such events as the 5000, 10,000 and marathon are not Olympic events and therefore not as widely contested as shorter distances.

With women's distance races on the track at a standstill, it is understandable that women's road racing was less than a popular sport prior to the 1960s. Ken Foreman, longtime women's distance coach from Seattle reports that the Scots, Welsh and English did offer cross country and road racing for women in the 1920s through the 1940s. In the United States, however, there was no organized road racing or cross country running for women until the 1960s. The first nationally-recognized cross country race for women (1.5 miles) was run around Seattle's Green Lake in 1965 with teenage half-mile sensation Marie Mulder the winner. Distance races on the track were even slower in coming; the first officially recorded three mile record was set in 1971 by Cheryl Bridges who ran 17:01.

Both off and on the track, women were stymied by AAU officials who felt that women were not capable of running long distances. Women were not only forbidden to compete in such races as the Boston Marathon, they were forbidden from competing in any race longer than 2.5 miles up until 1970. Women ran anyway, attracted to the road races which were starting to pick up steam in the mid-1960s.

Many women, competing strictly on their own—no coach, no club—were probably unaware of the AAU's ban on long distance races for women, unless, of course, the race officials took the AAU at its word and refused to let women run.

The big blow-up came in 1967 when Kathrine Switzer entered the males-only Boston Marathon, wearing an official number that she had received by signing up using her first initial instead of her first name. Even though another woman, Roberta Gibb Bingay, had successfully negotiated Boston the previous year in a very respectable 3:21, finishing 124th of 416 starters, no woman had ever tried to run officially. Race director Jock Semple was so ired by Switzer's entry that he tried to physically remove her from the course. Her massively-built boyfriend interceded and Switzer completed the race—as did Bingay (for the second time)—without incident. Pictures of the Switzer-Semple encounter flashed along the news wires and women's running suddenly had a heroine.

In other races, women were asked to start ten or fifteen

minutes before male runners. That tactic didn't always work. In an eight-mile race in Oregon, teenager Caroline Walker, who had set a world marathon best of 3:02:53 in 1970, beat the officials to the finish line. In the New York City Marathon of 1972 six women sat down on the starting line when the "women's gun" was fired. They started with the men but their times were never adjusted.

In areas where politics were not felt so heavily, men and women raced side-by-side, and in 1972 the AAU agreed to let women compete on an equal basis from the starting line to the finish line. Nonetheless, certain forms of discrimination in the sport persisted.

THEY ARE FRIENDS NOW, BUT IN 1967 BAA OFFICIALS ATTEMPTED TO STOP KATHRINE SWITZER FROM COMPETING IN THE BOSTON MARATHON.

While men enjoyed being able to compete within certain age divisions—allowing each runner a chance to compete with his peers and receive appropriate recognition—women often were forced to enter either a men's open division or a men's age-group division because there was no women's division, much less women's age group divisions. At this time, most women would have been pleased to have had just one division for women since the number of female entries did not warrant multiple age-group divisions.

In another instance of discrimination, women marathon runners were required to get a physical exam from their doctor (at no small cost) in order to enter a well-known West Coast marathon. Men were not required to have a physical.

Welcome or not, women kept running and competing, enough so that the AAU finally took them seriously, after previously dismissing them as a bunch of women "out for a lark." In 1974 the AAU actually was sanctioning and sponsoring women's marathon and 10,000 meter road racing championships.

In 1975 Ernst Van Aaken of West Germany organized the first women's international marathon. Since then, corporations and businesses have seen merit in sponsoring women's races and women in all parts of the United States have the opportunity to compete in women-only races, a thrilling experience for women who are used to being lost in the middle of the pack in other road races, rarely able to see the competition because the men outnumber the women by about ten to one in most races.

Even though women's races draw up to 4000 competitors and top runners are running under 2:40 in the marathon and 34:00 in the 10,000, international bodies have refused to recognize anything longer than 3000 meters for international track competition and 1500 meters for Olympic competition.

American women are fortunate since most high school programs offer a two-mile or 3000 meter race in track and/or a two-to-three mile cross country race. The 3000, 5000 and 10,000 are part of the collegiate track program, and national road racing championships are held at a variety of distances, as are a huge number of open races around the country.

Women's road racing is still in its infancy on a world-wide scene, but women on all continents are beginning to make inroads into male-dominated road races. Social and cultural mores will restrict progress in some countries, but the fact that women around the world are finding road racing to be a rewarding activity is reason to believe that the sport will continue to grow.

2
SELECTING RACES

With the current boom in commercial sponsorship of road races, it's not difficult for the road racer to find competition. What may be more difficult is finding a comprehensive schedule of races around which to arrange a training schedule.

The Road Runners Club of America offers regional race information and can put you in touch with your region's director of communications. Some regional Long Distance Running Committees of the Amateur Athletic Union also publish long distance racing schedules for their AAU members. National publications such as *Runner's World* and *Running Times* publish racing calendars in each issue, although without any kind of comprehensive long-range listings.

Track clubs and road running clubs often publish newsletters and those newsletters may be your best source of local race information. If you're new to an area, check with your Chamber of Commerce for the name of a local running club. Sporting goods stores are often another important source of race information; many display a notice board of race announcements. Once you've attended one race in a new community you're sure to find other runners with knowledge of local races. Race promoters often will distribute fliers about their race at other local races.

Although the big-name races draw the most publicity and may be the ones where you want to make your big effort, various communities have low-key weekly or monthly races, often using the same course or a set number of courses, repeating them on an annual basis.

It may be to your advantage to compete in these races regularly. The fields generally will be small enough that you can get an accurate time, entry fees will be low and you can measure your fitness by comparing your times to past performances on the same course. You'll also be giving moral support to the local groups which will be sponsoring races year after year when the one-shot, highly-promoted races have gone the way of the buffalo.

Road races range from half-mile fun runs to relays around Lake Tahoe, from races up 14,000-foot Pike's Peak to the Boston Marathon. They range from ubiquitous 10,000 meter races to seldom run 100-milers. You can also select some fun racing combinations, such as Ride and Tie Races where two teammates (plus a horse) alternate running and riding over a given distance. You can enter biathlons (running and swimming), triathlons (biking, running, swimming), or various other combinations of running, canoeing, biking, swimming, skiing or whatever someone thinks up. Sometimes you'll do the races in relay fashion, at other times you may have the option to do all segments of the race yourself.

Most road racers though, will content themselves to pounding the fast macadam roads, looking for the perfect course (slightly downhill), the perfect day (cool, overcast, trailing wind) and the perfect feeling of fitness (light weight, three months of 100-mile weeks, perfect health). Naturally, most of us are still looking.

What does the serious road racer look for in a race?

Certain factors are obvious: an accurate course, an accurate time and place, adequate aid stations when appropriate, and the promise of favorable weather conditions.

COURSE ACCURACY

You've run an impressive time—almost too good to be true. What's more, so did everyone else you knew in the race. Were the conditions perfect that day? Or was the course short?

Determining the accuracy of a road course is difficult unless the race director can assure you that he measured the course with a calibrated wheel. Marathon courses, which didn't become a standardized length until the 1920s, are generally certified, which means that the race director has sent in his measurements, calibrations and computations to Ted Corbitt, Chairman of the AAU Standards Committee, who gives official certification to the course. Corbitt also certifies courses of other road racing distances (which *Running Times* lists in its calendar). Your chances of finding a certified marathon course far exceed your chances of finding a certified course at any other distance, particularly due to the greater importance of the marathon distance for those runners trying to meet standards to qualify for the Olympic marathon trial, and partially due to the fact that promoters of shorter races often view the event as a recreational contest, being more interested in large numbers of runners rather than accurate times and distances.

If the race director can't give you a satisfactory answer about the accuracy of the course, you have several options: you can measure the course on a bike with a calibration device (available from Clain Jones, 3717 Wildwood Dr., Endwell, N.Y. 13760). This process involves measuring at least a half-mile with a steel tape on a straight road, then riding your bike over the measured distance to determine the proper calibration (i.e., 760 revolutions equals one mile). For a slightly less accurate measurement (not good enough for certification), you can drive your car over the same tape-measured half-mile several times to check your odometer's accuracy. With the odometer method you can drive the road course, checking your odometer and then multipying by a correcting factor, as determined by driving the steel-taped segment. You may discover that when your odometer reads "one mile", you've actually covered .94 mile. Therefore you can multiply the distance shown on your odometer (i.e., six miles), by .94 to find the actual distance, (6 x .94 - 5.64 miles). Biking the distance with a calibrated device will measure the course within inches, but the odometer measurement is probably good enough for you, the racer, to satisfy yourself that the course was or wasn't a quarter-mile short.

A third alternative to measuring a course—and good also for measuring your training courses—is to investigate geological survey maps, most readily available in the geography departments of colleges and universities. The maps are very detailed and can give you not only relatively accurate distances, but elevation information as well.

IS THE TIME ACCURATE? DID YOU GET A PLACE?

Once you've satisfied yourself about the accuracy of a course, how do you find out if your time is accurate? If you're one of the leaders, or the first woman finisher, you probably don't need to worry. Otherwise, have a friend time you or time yourself. The smaller the field, the better your chances are of getting an accurate time and place. Some race officials simply give up after the first 300 or 400 runners come thundering across the line. Find out before the race if someone will be reading times aloud at the finish line or if a digital clock will be displayed at the finish. Often you're too tired to look at a clock or listen for a time, but try to stay alert and if possible, clue in a friend to watch or listen for your time when you finish. It may be the only time you'll get.

In large fields your friend may not be able to help. He may not even see you at the finish if you're racing in with a mob. If you want to be absolutely certain of your time, time yourself with a stop watch, preferably one you can wear on your wrist. As for your place, you may or may not receive that information, depending on how well-organized the officials are. You can help though, by staying in line through the chute, by wearing your official number (and being officially entered), and by completing any finish line procedures necessary, such as turning in a name-tag, number or card with a finish number. And steer clear of the finish area once you've finished, to help cut down on the confusion.

AID STATIONS

Aid stations should be a requirement for every race longer than 10,000 meters, and would be advisable even for races shorter than 10,000 meters in hot weather. Check with race officials ahead of time to find out if and when aid will be available (this information should be on the entry information form) and what will be offered (water, Gatorade, your own specialty, sponges). Fluid intake is discussed in a later chapter—but you should know ahead of time what aid will be offered and what aid you should arrange for yourself, whether it's having a friend hand you a squeeze bottle of water every three miles or leaving your own special preparation at the official aid station. If you do have a special drink you may be best off to give the drink to a friend (your handler), to avoid any mix-ups at the official aid stations when you frantically try to identify your container without losing time. Some people fasten balloons or paint their containers with bright, identifiable colors, but in races with large fields, such efforts may not be sufficient.

WEATHER

Racing under different weather conditions is addressed elsewhere but in selecting a race, take into consideration the starting time and approximate finish time. What will the temperature be during that time period? Will the course be shady or out in the blazing sun? Can you expect drifts of snow and 25 mph wind gusts during the race? Will the humidity be 90 percent?

Check the average weather conditions of the race site for that particular race date if you're unfamiliar with the area. Avoid summer races which start during mid-day. Even if you're heat acclimatized, you won't be able to race to your potential at 1:00 p.m. if the temperature is in the 90s. If you're looking for fast times, select cooperative racing weather.

Other considerations in race selection may not be so obvious. Have you given thought to the course itself? The cost of the entry fee? Your ability to run competitively in a given field?

THE COURSE

The more you race, the better you'll know your own strengths and weaknesses. Do hills sap your strength or give you an advantage over the field? Are you prone to twisting your ankle when you run over uneven ground or do you feel like you're flying when you race over varied surfaces? Do you feel confident racing at high altitude even if you're not acclimatized? Do you enjoy speeding away on long, flat stretches, or do you find that they cause you to lose your concentration?

Certainly not every race course is going to suit you ideally, but when selecting your most important race of the season, choose a course which will be to your advantage, based on your racing strengths. Being familiar with the course also will be to your advantage during the race. You'll know what to expect, how to pace yourself to meet the demands of the terrain and where to make tactical moves.

ENTRY FEES

The cost of race entry fees has increased almost as much as the number of runners entering the races. The average entry fee, for short and long distance races alike, seems to be creeping towards $5.00 per race (some are asking $10.00), which for the average runner who may compete in 15 or 20 races a year, can add up to more than the cost of a year's supply of running shoes.

It may seem overly pecuniary or miserly, but before you decide to pay five bucks to enter a race, ask yourself just what you're getting in return.

Are t-shirts being offered to all finishers? Do you really want another t-shirt? Those first few shirts which you wore like badges of honor have probably grown faded by now and sit at the bottom of the pile in your bulging dresser drawer.

Some race directors are wisely offering the runner a choice on the t-shirts. If you enter the race you can buy a commemorative t-shirt for a couple of dollars, more if you are not entered in the race. In other instances, race directors have iron-on race decals—much less expensive than t-shirts—which you can do with as you please.

If t-shirts are being offered, figure that they cost roughly $3.00, much less if they're mass produced for a series of races being held around the country under the sponsorship of one group. What's happening with your other $2.00?

If police have to be hired, toilet facilities paid for, a hall rented, aid stations provided, results mailed and merchandise prizes or trophies given, you can probably assume that your money is spent on legitimate expenses. If, however, none or few of the above amenities are being provided, you have a right to question the high entry fee.

You may be quite willing to pay an extra dollar if the money is going to a charitable cause or to the sponsoring group, but race sponsors have an obligation to let the runner know if the race is being run as a benefit for one group or another.

The big business sponsorship of races clouds the issue somewhat. On the one hand, race sponsors are willing to pour thousands of dollars into races in terms of publicity and promotion, in order to draw several thousand runners. If the race draws, say, 4,000 runners at $5.00 a head, that's a tidy sum of $20,000 in entry fees. If there is a profit after expenses are paid, who gets it? Is the sponsor company actually making money or breaking even and at the same time reaping the benefits of having the sponsor's name emblazoned on the chests of 4,000 runners? Consider also the additional publicity the race itself draws. Are you, the runner, being used unwittingly to advertise a product?

Concern has been expressed about the suitability of certain companies to be race sponsors. Is it appropriate for a product—such as diet pop—which is labelled "may be dangerous to your health", to be associated with the health and fitness of a runner? You are healthy and fit because you run, not because you drink diet pop, yet if you ran in a race sponsored by Diet Pepsi (and sanctioned by the AAU) you probably signed a release form which gave the manufacturers of the product the right to use pictures of you in advertising their product . . . despite the fact that the AAU forbids such a practice.

It may not make any difference to you if a race sponsor earns his livelihood through diet pop, whiskey, cigarettes, candy or trendy sports clothing. But in a time when we are fortunate enough to have a choice of races in which to compete, you can be discriminating as to where you choose to lay down your $5.00 entry fee.

Another philosophical consideration for the road racer—especially the one on a limited budget—is the fact that he may be subsidizing other runners. Some runners enjoy having a chance to rub shoulders with a Frank Shorter or a Bill Rodgers or a Gayle Barron. And they're willing to pay for the privilege. Other racers may be less happy to help pay expenses to bring in a big-name runner if he's there only as window-dressing rather than to compete. The racer may also dislike subsidizing expenses for a big-name, but out-of-shape, runner to compete when there are dozens of fit no-name runners with similar credentials who would appreciate the chance to be flown out to a big race.

Be selective in your choice of races. If you feel that race entry fees are sky-high and that you're being asked to pay for things you either don't want or don't even receive (i.e., adequate aid stations, official results), then boycott such races and support the smaller races which may charge only a nominal fee and offer no more than ribbons for prizes. Although financial disclosures have not yet become a major issue in road racing, you do have a right to ask the meet director where your money is going.

In most cases, little or no money is being made by the people organizing races, most of whom are volunteers. The majority of these people are trying to break even and provide you with a service. So be polite, but if the price seems high, ask questions.

CAN YOU BE COMPETITIVE?

When selecting a race you should consider your chances of being competitive in the field. Will you have to run 90 percent of the distance with no one in sight, fore or aft, because the field is so small? Or will you have to race in a field so jammed that you can barely find enough room to run, let alone race?

And what do you do when 1,000 people converge on an aid station within two minutes?

If you're entering a race with a small field you'll obviously have a better chance of winning the race, or your division, or finishing in the top 10 or 20 or whatever, if that is meaningful to you. But can you sustain a pace when you're by yourself? Or are you the type of racer who needs someone breathing down your neck, or the sight of another runner to pass, to keep your adrenalin up and your legs flying? Or do you prefer to enter the race with a friend of near-equal ability and cruise through the event at a pre-determined pace, working together but not racing against each other?

Larger fields may give you the competition you hunger for, the chance to really test yourself against a representative field of competitors of your ability. But too-large fields may actually slow you down, especially if you're a middle-of-the-pack runner. Remember that it may take you minutes to cross the starting line and minutes more to gear down from 10:00 miles to 7:00 miles because of the press of the crowd. What do you hope to accomplish in the race? Are you running it for the pleasure of running with thousands of other people? Are you seriously trying to race the distance and get an accurate time and place? Unless you're in the top 10

THE FIRST STEP IN ACHIEVING GOALS IS TO SELECT RACES WITH CARE.

percent of the field (in races of 2,000-plus runners), you're unlikely to be able to run hard the whole way. You are going to get a slow start and you may have to wait to cross the finish line. Even if you are among the top five or ten percent of the finishers in your class (excluding the open class) you won't have a chance to race the whole way, much less identify your competition. For this reason, women and masters should be encouraged to peak for races designated as only for their particular group, so that they can experience the true feeling of racing and competition that top male road racers feel. How many women or masters runners ever get the feeling of leading the pack, setting the pace, or of actually seeing how far ahead or behind the rest of the competitive field is?

More races are starting to limit fields, and for this the runner should be thankful. If you're very serious about running a race—the big one for you—you're going to know about it long in advance in order to train for it. You should be able to get your entry in on time and not have to worry about thousands of last-minute entries cramming the field. Ideally, races with limited fields should limit the fields on a first-come-first-entered basis, so that there is a normal distribution of runners. Races, such as Boston, which impose qualifying standards have several problems. First, they inadvertently invite a small number of liars, cheats and scoundrels who enter without legitimate qualifying times. Secondly, they can never put a tight limit on the number of entries. Seemingly, the tougher the standard, the harder people try to make it and the more they succeed. Thirdly, by having a qualifying time, the sponsors are truncating the normal distribution of fast and slow runners. Instead of having 10 to 20 percent of the field running faster than 2:40 for the marathon, 50 to 60 percent running between 2:40 and 3:40 and 20 to 40 percent running slower than 3:40, Boston race officials suddenly find themselves with close to 80 or 90 percent of the runners running between 2:40 and 3:50. That can mean the difference between 1,000 people crossing the finish line in an hour and nearly 2,000 people crossing the line in that time.

At Boston in 1975, with a field of 2,000-plus, 114 runners

bettered 2:30. Then came 774 runners from 2:30 to 3:00; 930 finishers, or half the field finished in the next half-hour. Boston officials stop the clock at 3:30, but it can be assumed that another few hundred runners trickled in between 3:30 and 4:30.

Of course, if you've run a 10,000 meter race with 4,000 runners, all finishing within an hour, you may find the finish line at Boston to be relatively deserted. Be that as it may, there is no doubt that race officials have a much more difficult time giving you an official place and time when people are finishing close together. And likewise, out on the course, you're going to have an easier time getting aid if there are fewer people converging on the aid station.

RACING INFORMATION

AAU House, 3400 W. 86th St., Indianapolis, Ind. 46269 can put you in touch with your local AAU organization. When you get your AAU card and have signed up for long distance running as your sport, some associations will send you a schedule of races in your region.

Ted Corbitt, Chairman, AAU Standards Committee, Apt. 8H, Section 4, 150 West 225th St., N.Y., N.Y. 10463. Corbitt oversees course certification.

National Jogging Association, P.O. Box 57326, Washington D.C. 20037 is a clearinghouse for information about jogging.

Road Runners' Club of America, c/o President Jeff Darman, 2727 Devonshire Pl., N.W., Washington D.C. 20008 offers regional race information and can give you the name of your region's directory of communications.

Runner's World Fun-Run, Box 366, Mountain View, Calif. 94042 can provide you with a list of fun runs throughout the United States.

RUNNING AND TRACK PUBLICATIONS

Athletica, P.O. Box CP4981, Vancouver, B.C. V6B4A6 is a Canadian track and field magazine which covers some long distance races.

ALL ABOUT ROAD RACING

Athletics Weekly, 344 High St., Rochester, Kent, England covers track and field and road racing in the British Commonwealth.

Runner's World, Box 366, Mountain View, Calif. 94042 is aimed at the beginning runner and the long distance runner. Nationwide (but sketchy) calendar and results.

The Runner, 1 Park Ave., New York, N.Y. 10016. Slick running magazine covering wide range of running-related topics.

Running Times, 12808 Occoquan Rd., Woodbridge, Va. 22192 covers road racing. Good running calendar and results section.

Track and Field News, Box 296, Los Altos, Calif. 94022 covers top national and international track and field and some road racing.

Women's Track World, P.O. Box 886, Mentone, Calif. 92359, formerly *Women's Track and Field World,* has resurfaced after ceasing publication in 1976. The magazine covers women's track and field, national and international, and some road racing.

GOVERNING ORGANIZATIONS

Amateur Athletic Union (AAU), 3400 W 86th St., Indianapolis, Ind. 46269 governs most amateur sports in the United States and sponsors national championships in track and field, road races (including marathon) and cross country.

International Olympic Committee, Chateau de Vidy, CH-1007, Lausanne, Switzerland. Governs Olympic sports.

International Amateur Athletic Federation, 162 Upper Richmond Road, Putney, London, S.W. 15 2SL, England. Governs international amateur sports.

ATHLETIC MEDICINE

Sheehan, George, *The Encyclopedia of Athletic Medicine,* World Publications, Mountain View, CA.

Subotnick, Steven, *The Running Foot Doctor.* World Publications, Mountain View, Ca.

HISTORY

Chodes, John, *Corbitt: The Story of Ted Corbitt, Long*

Distance Runner, Tafnews Press, Los Altos, Ca.

Schaap, Richard, *An Illustrated History of the Olympics,* Knopf, N.Y., N.Y. (The *Reader's Guide* in your local library can direct you to magazine accounts of early day road racing in periodicals such as *Collier's, Outing, Literary Digest, Outlook.*)

NUTRITION

Smith, Nathan J., *Food for Sport,* Bull Publishing Co., Palo Alto, Ca.

Whitney, Eleanor Noss and Hamilton, Eva May Nunnelley, *Understanding Nutrition* (college text), West Publishing Co., St. Paul, Minn.

RACE ORGANIZATION

Road Runners Club of America Handbook, published by RRCA, Washington, D.C.

TRAINING

Costill, David L., *What Research Tells the Coach About Distance Running.* AAPHER, Washington, D.C.

Costill, David L., *A Scientific Approach to Distance Running,* Tafnews Press, Los Altos, Ca.

Doherty, John Kenneth, *Track and Field Omnibook,* Tafmop Publishers, Swarthmore, Pa.

Lydiard, Arthur, *Running the Lydiard Way,* World Publications, Mountain View, Ca.

Murray, Chris, "The Middle and Long Distances," *Championship Track and Field for Women* (Wilt, Ecker and Hay, editors), Parker Publishing, Co., Inc., West Nyack, N.Y.

Watts, D.C.V. and Wilson, Harry, *Middle and Long Distance, Marathon and Steeplechase,* British Amateur Athletic Board, London.

GENERAL INTEREST

Anderson, Bob and Henderson, Joe, *Guide to Distance Running,* Runner's World, Mountain View, Ca.

Burger, Robert, *Jogger's Catalog, "the sourcebook for runners,"* M. Evans & Co., Inc., N.Y., N.Y.

The Complete Runner. Editors of Runner's World, World Publications, Mountain View, Ca.

Fixx, James, *The Complete Book of Running,* Random House, N.Y., N.Y.

Henderson, Joe, *The Complete Marathoner,* World Publications, Mountain View, Ca.

3
TRAINING FOR ROAD RACING

As you change from a fitness runner or fun runner into a competitive runner, your reasons for running change, too.

For the fun runner, daily running is an important end in itself. The ultimate reward may be fitness, but the daily rewards are the feeling of well-being, a sense of accomplishment (and therefore an improved self-image) and, perhaps, the companionship of other runners.

As you become a racer, these daily achievements may take a back seat. Daily running becomes a means to an end—road racing. You still get the daily return, but you have a new goal. As a road runner your running will become more sophisticated, more precise. You'll be "training."

HOW TO START TRAINING

The minute you begin preparing for racing, you begin training. Your training can be complicated or simple. It may depend on the races you're going to train for.

The simplest things you can do are run farther, and run faster. The proper mixture is the hard part.

It is best to start with some general guidelines before trying to make specific programs.

TRAIN, DON'T STRAIN: MAXIMUM vs. OPTIMUM

The "train, don't strain" concept was first espoused in the U.S. by Bill Bowerman, the former University of Oregon men's track coach. It is a concept which is exceedingly difficult to believe in.

Our interpretation of this concept involves working at your optimum level, not at your maximum level. Your goal is to do what's best for you, not to do the most you think you can possibly handle. For some people maximum and optimum are the same, but not for many. The runner who can do 110 miles a week may be better off doing 90 instead. The man who can blitz through a 10-mile training run in 58 minutes might need to do just that now and then. He may be better off, though, doing most of his 10-milers slower. He should be training, not straining.

As long as your heart rate is 125 beats per minute or more while you're running, you're achieving a training effect. This minimum rate is usually achieved at a conversational pace which would pass Bowerman's "talk test." You pass the test if you're running at a speed at which you can carry on a conversation. Getting to that level is the goal of the beginning fitness runner. For a racer it's a level at which he can comfortably train. He can put in a lot of miles at that speed, achieve a great deal and not strain at all until he's covered many miles.

MODERATION

Many very old people claim they got that way by being moderate in all things. The runner who trains moderately may take some time to achieve his goal but he stands a good chance of succeeding. The runner who overtrains may find success more quickly—or he may get hurt, get sick, or quit. Chances of illness or early "retirement" are decreased through moderate training. Give yourself enough time in your training plan, so that you don't need a crash program to get ready for a race. Crash programs rarely work. Moderate, planned training programs do.

UNDERTRAINING VS. OVERTRAINING

Your training goal is to do the optimum amount and kind of running for you. Athletes who are smart or lucky do the optimum. Olympic gold medal winners do the optimum. Those who never make it to the Games even though they should, often have tried to do the maximum.

If you don't know what's right for you, do less. It's better to be undertrained than overtrained. The undertrained runner will make steady progress through a season or series of races and will run his best in the most important race at the end of the series, as he should. The overtrained runner may well run impressive times early, but in all likelihood will crash and burn before he gets to the big race. He might have a few weeks of greatness followed by a period of injury, maybe an illness, then a crash program to get ready for the big race.

The undertrained runner will run his best effort in the final, most important race—and his appetite will be whetted for more, because he knows next time he can do a little more running and maybe he can train a little smarter. After a deserved rest, he'll be ready to go again.

HARD/EASY METHOD

Most of us were raised to believe in the Puritan work ethic: there's virtue in hard work. Therefore, we reason there must be more virtue in even more work. In running, fortunately, there is also virtue in rest. A runner who trains hard must also rest. One is as necessary as the other for success.

Bowerman's simple hard day/easy day method has this

concept built in. Train hard on Monday, run easily on Tuesday, so you can go hard again on Wednesday. It's not a perfect method but it helps prevent overtraining. Some runners may wipe themselves out on Monday, and be unable to do anything but jog on Tuesday and Wednesday. Others may not train that hard on Monday and will go only a little easier on Tuesday.

The easy day, for some people, is a built-in reward. You can really hammer on Monday if you'll get to go for an easy run in the park on Tuesday. And you'll be refreshed and eager to work hard by Wednesday.

PROGRESSIVE OVERLOAD

If you work a muscle harder than it's used to being worked, and let it rest, it will get stronger. Muscles and systems adapt as a result of the stresses placed upon them. They adapt best under a program that is progressively more demanding.

Thus, by training moderately and letting your body rest, and by gradually increasing your running (faster, farther), you'll get fitter and fitter, and you'll race faster and faster.

These guidelines seem to emphasize rest, moderation and easy days. That's only because the tendency of the hungry runner is not to do too little but to try to do too much. The smart runner must also be a tough runner. He may have to face workouts he doesn't want to do. He's going to spend some time being very uncomfortable and some other times in pain, pure and simple. But if he does it with a plan in mind, a plan that has built-in easy days, it will be bearable, maybe even fun, and probably successful.

COMPONENTS OF TRAINING

What is successful? What are your goals? Those topics are covered elsewhere in depth, a bit philosophically. For our purposes, let's say that success is running faster than you've ever run for a given distance or a given course. What should you do to achieve this goal?

SPECIFICITY

The first thing you should consider altering is your training load so that you train more specifically for your goal, which is a successful race or a successful series of races. An important factor here is specificity ("specific-ness"). Your training should become more and more specific to the race you'll be running. Specificity of training implies that you become good at the things you practice. Therefore, your practices should be very similar to the actual event or parts of it. This is critically important in skilled athletic events. It is also important in repetitive athletic events such as running. If you're going to train for a 30-kilometer race, some of your training runs must be much farther but not as fast as they would be if you were training for a 10-kilometer race. If the race is in the hills, you should do a part of your training on hills. If the race is at 3:00 p.m. on a day in July in Kansas, you'd better do some heat training.

The specific requirements of a race tell us what must be emphasized. This does not mean you should train with a precise race-oriented goal in mind every day. Many training sessions remain general in their content and objective and are almost universally used. The long run, usually on Sunday, is a staple of many runners' plans and is non-specific until it is increased in length to prepare for a particularly long race.

MILEAGE

As you become a serious road racer your first inclination may be to increase your mileage. Your reasoning will be "more is better," which is true up to a point.

Counting miles is not a great way to gauge your training. It is, however, the easiest measurable way. You must remember, however, that 50 miles of easy running each week is not equal to 50 miles of track work, or fartlek or high altitude training. Henry Rono's 80-mile week is not necessarily of the same intensity as your 80-mile week.

Counting miles, nevertheless, is a place to start.

Some runners measure their favorite courses quite accurately. Others simply estimate a distance after timing a run several times with a wristwatch.

In discussions of appropriate mileage, let's assume that a runner is doing a mixture of intensities, and that well over half of the total mileage is steady running at a moderate tempo.

The lower mileage limit for a racer should be in the range of 35 miles per week, at which one could race effectively up to 10 kilometers. To race farther you generally must train farther. To race 25 kilometers a runner should do at least 45 miles per week. The marathon requires a rock-bottom mileage of 55 miles per week.

The better prepared you are for any of these distances, the more enjoyable the race will be and the less it will take out of you during and after the race.

The marathon in particular must be adequately prepared for. If you do not do the work ahead of time, the race will feel like a death march and the marathon will be worse than you ever dreamed it could be. The only way to run a marathon is to run it well. And that means putting in a lot of miles over many weeks to prepare.

The mileages quoted above are approximate and they are the minimums. An experienced road racer with several years of background will do 70 to 90 miles a week, perhaps even more. Some people still swear by 100 miles a week, every week.

Again, what kind of running you do is as important as how much you do. There are several standard types of training from which you can pick and choose.

LONG SLOW DISTANCE (LSD)

Long, slow distance running in its original form was a training method espoused by Joe Henderson. It involved lots of mileage at a very slow pace. Its virtues were that it seemed to cause very few injuries and that it was not stressful on the minds of some runners. Few serious runners actually have used pure LSD. Our meaning for the term LSD is easy, steady-paced

52

running. It's the base from which you build your program. You start a training plan with LSD after coming back from an injury or illness or any enforced layoff. You run easily until you feel ready to add other types of training to your program. Easy day runs and morning runs often will fit this description, as will many of your long, weekend runs. The first few times you go out to cover a greater distance than you've ever gone before, you'll do LSD. Later, when you're stronger, your long runs may be at a faster tempo.

INTERVAL TRAINING

True interval training has a precise use and is very regimented. In general use, however, interval training or "running intervals" has come to mean any repetitions of timed distances. Intervals are usually done in a track session and may be quite uniform (12 x 440 in 75 seconds, with 1:00 jog between). Or they may be varied (3 x 220 in 35 seconds with 220 jog, jog 660 on the grass, 1 x mile in 5:10, walk 880, 4 x 440 in 68 seconds with a 440 jog, jog 880 on the grass, 5 x 165 striding the first 110 and sprinting the last 55 and jogging 165 between).

Interval training lets you run at race pace or faster many times during a workout. You become more mechanically efficient at faster speeds. You learn to differentiate various tempos because you can check yourself on every lap. You learn to cope with the pain of a fast tempo.

It appears that the more interval training you do, the faster you become fit. You don't get to a higher level than you would using other methods or a mixture of methods, you just get there faster.

Interval training, though, takes its toll. It can be a harsh, burdensome method if used alone as it was in the 1950s and early 1960s by most track runners. A mixture of intervals and other running is currently in favor.

You may find you need to do interval training, love to do it, or can find other things to substitute for it. Even more than most kinds of running, intervals require training partners, so seek them out. The stress of interval training is great. Having someone else running with you distracts you enough to make the training much easier.

Keeping in mind the specificity guideline: interval training is most important if you're racing at short distances. If you're a man trying to run 10 kilometers in 31:00 (5:00 minutes per mile), interval training is one of the few ways you can run that pace in a workout. So you may do 15 x 440 in 72 seconds, or 6 x 1320 in 3:42, or 4 x 1¼ miles in 6:15 (or something similar but more varied). The shorter the race, the more useful interval training is.

Also, the faster you are, the more useful interval training is. A 2:15 marathoner can step onto the track and do repetitions near 5:00 mile pace—running that is specific to his race.

The slower you are in absolute terms, and the longer the distance of the race, the less you'll need to do intervals. As an extreme example, the 3:30 marathoner races at 8:00 per mile and he does a great deal of his steady running at the same pace. Yet the same person may want to run a 10 kilometer race in 43:00, faster than 7:00 pace. Therefore he may want to do interval running that includes repeated miles at 6:30 pace.

FARTLEK

Fartlek (Swedish for "speed play") is a creative type of running in which you vary your speed as you wish during a workout. Classically, it's done in an aesthetic setting such as a park, forest trail or golf course. You do what your mood and the lay of the land dictate, including sprinting, striding, jogging and walking.

You're supposed to finish a fartlek session envigorated rather than exhausted. Some runners are fully capable of this. Others may have difficulty with such a free lance workout since it requires creativity, yet discipline enough to make a true workout of it. Some people are frustrated because they can't measure it. Others are overjoyed because it's a frolic.

If you're comfortable with fartlek, do it. It you can't get

in the mood for it after giving it a fair chance, do other things or alter it to meet your needs. Some runners do interval sessions in the woods without a stopwatch, letting effort dictate the tempo.

HILLS

One must train on hills to become a good racer on hills. Uphill running requires power, like that of a sprinter. It requires a sprint motion with vigorous arm-pumping, full extension of the legs on pushoff. A runner must not let himself bend excessively at the waist because this forces him out of the power position. Instead, bend forward from the ankle. Look at the top of the hill or up the hill.

If you are not a power runner, get to the top of the hill as best you can using proper style, and gain back what you lose by going hard down hill. (Great downhill runners claim they can keep their torsos perpendicular to the downhill surface.) Try not to lean back or land hard on your heels when running fast. Try to attack on the way down a hill, but keep in control of your body. You may find yourself decelerating with your entire lower body as you stay perpendicular to the surface with your upper body.

Remember, all the speed you get going down hill is virtually free due to gravity. You worked hard to get to the top. Use the down hill as well as you can, expending as little energy as you can to take advantage of gravity.

SUSTAINED RUNS

Sustained runs are a key part of the road runner's training. There is no widely accepted work which describes this type of running, probably because no one has advocated it as a "method" like LSD or interval training.

A sustained run is a hard training run on the road, or one in which you find yourself having to make a conscious effort to sustain the pace.

You probably have your own word for such running. Some

runners classify running in three ways: 1) easy—a purposefully slow pace, 2) moderate—a normal pace in which there is no conscious effort to go fast or slow, 3) hard—a pace which feels fast and quickly requires an effort to maintain it.

The hard or sustained run may be close to race tempo, close enough that you can only hold it for a fraction of the actual race distance. A fit marathon runner, for example, might have difficulty running more than 10 miles at race pace in a workout.

The ability to run fast in a training session varies among runners. Some people can train very fast and race fast, too. Others train very fast but race poorly. A third type of runner can't run fast in a workout but is able to hold a pace in a race that is much faster than you'd expect. If you're the first or third type of runner, you're all right. If you fit the second description, be more moderate in your training and save your racing for race day.

Sustained runs should be planned, or at least adjusted for. If you're going to do a moderately paced 10-mile run but you feel great, can't hold yourself back, and end up hammering it, you should be prepared to alter your next day or two if you're exhausted after your hard run.

The better way is to plan a sustained run and stick to your plan. You need to allow appropriate rest depending on the length and effort of the run.

You may find a hard one-hour run or a hard run over a known loop is enough, without need to time it or measure the distance. At other times you may want to do something more formal. Some training groups have accurately measured road courses with each mile or kilometer marked on the pavement. You can plan a particular pace for a specific distance and get intermediate splits along the way. It need not be an all-out effort. The race-like atmosphere, with a planned sub-maximal effort, should provide more than enough incentive to achieve a sustained effort you'll be proud of.

The distance can be as far as 10 to 12 miles and include a steady pace throughout. Or you might try a moderate start, then a hard tempo for several miles and a maximal mile to the finish. A third variation might be putting the very hard mile in the middle of the run, simulating a tactical race burst.

You can vary these runs for your specific needs and abilities.

Sustained runs are the most race-specific type of training you'll do. At various times you can run at or near race tempo for an extended period of time. This will help you mechanically, physiologically and psychologically. It will help you "groove" the pace as well as force you to cope with discomfort over many minutes as you must in a race.

PLANNING A TRAINING PROGRAM

You must have a plan. Serious athletes are goal-oriented athletes. The more specific the goals, the better.

With a specific goal you can put together a specific program. Here, personality makes the great difference among runners. One person may know exactly what he wants to do a month ahead of time. He may need to have a plan on paper simply to get himself out the door to start a workout. Other people may have only a general idea of what they want to do. They might decide what type of training session to do while changing clothes or walking to the door. Many methods have worked. We suggest you try the more specific plan first and retreat to something less specific if you must in order to feel comfortable.

Whether or not you write down your training plan in advance is up to you. However, it is important to keep a log of the training you've actually done. Record your daily mileage, the kind or intensity of the workout, race results, injuries, illness and on a weekly basis, your weight. Your training log will be invaluable as you set out to plan future training programs, to figure out what went wrong, and what went right.

Using the guidelines discussed earlier, you can create your training plan by using a mixture of training methods. Most world class athletes are using a combination of fast runs, intervals, and fartlek, with moderate and easy runs as needed. Variety is an important factor, both to maintain interest and to hit all the bases, covering all possible needs.

What you do will depend on your own situation. What time of day can you train? Can you run twice a day? Do you have access to a track, trails, golf course or park? Do you have people to run with? What's the weather like? Considering these and other factors, you should alter anything written here to fit your own experience, environment and interests.

Remembering the guidelines and types of running previously mentioned, you might follow a schedule like this:

Monday	Light run
Tuesday	Sustained run
Wednesday	Light run
Thursday	Fartlek
Friday	Light run
Saturday	Long run
Sunday	Light run
Monday	Moderate run
Tuesday	Light run
Wednesday	Interval workout
Thursday	Light run.
Friday	Fartlek
Saturday	Light run
Sunday	Sustained (timed) run

As you see, every other day is a recovery day and a variety of hard sessions are planned. It is a fourteen day cycle which does not fit some people's schedules since hard days are on Tuesday, Thursday and Saturday the first week, and Monday, Wednesday, Friday and Sunday the second week.

A seven day cycle might look like this:

Monday	Light run
Tuesday	Fartlek or intervals
Wednesday	Light run
Thursday	Sustained run
Friday	Light run
Saturday	Light or moderate run
Sunday	Long run

Morning runs (or a second daily run) can be added to this

schedule if you're up to it. Some people find that a light morning run is invigorating. Others simply are not "morning people." Still others do not have the time to run in the morning. A light run in the morning is an easy way to make your weekly mileage look impressive, although its value is debatable. In most basic terms, your objective in training is to spend a lot of time with your pulse elevated. Morning runs will give you a couple more hours of easy running each week and therefore will help you get fit. If you feel more and more exhausted in doing them, however, you may be overtraining.

In keeping with gradual increases in your training, you might try two morning runs a week. You'll see quickly if it's for you or not, and adjust accordingly.

The schedules above purposely list no mileage. Each has a different ability and need for work and a different running background. It is impossible to write a specific all-purpose training schedule that will be appropriate for each and every runner. Some ambitious runners make the mistake of trying to emulate someone else's training program, figuring that "if this program made so-and-so a 2:15 marathoner, it will make me one too."

Each runner must experiment with his training. Try some of this and some of that. Find out if you can handle intervals, fartlek and sustained runs of various sorts. Your own past experience is your best indicator of what you do. Just keep in mind the original guidelines—moderation, optimum vs. maximum—and keep learning about yourself.

Realizing that the less experienced road racer may have no competitive background, in either track or long distance running, and no idea of where he fits in the spectrum of fitness which determines the intensity of training one will do, we offer the following hypothetical cases to demonstrate different levels of training. These schedules are not meant to be copied by any runner who fits the case description, but they may help you determine your own training program.

Runner #1: A male runner, late 20s, 18 months of running background, has lost 10 pounds, is at a reasonable running weight now. Began with jogging and built up to 35 miles per week of steady running. Has run in several fun runs, can do four miles in 28 to 30 minutes. Wants to run close to 7:00 pace for races up to 10 miles; would like to run first marathon in six months.

This runner should concentrate on building mileage to a minimum of 55 miles per week with at least two runs 20 miles or longer. During the first three months of training the runner can concentrate on racing shorter distances while gradually increasing mileage. During the second three month period the emphasis will switch to mileage in preparation for the marathon.

Month 1: Increase mileage on weekly basis: 35 miles the first week, 40 miles the second week, 40 miles the third week, 45 miles the fourth week. A typical week's workout might be as follows:

Monday	3 miles easy
Tuesday	8 miles, pushing hard the last 4 miles
Wednesday	3 miles easy
Thursday	7 miles including light fartlek
Friday	3 miles easy
Saturday	5 miles easy or moderate
Sunday	10 to 12 miles easy
Total:	39 to 41 miles

Comments: This runner's easy days are token runs because the hard days are quite strenuous for a runner at this fitness level. The Saturday or Sunday runs may become race days for this runner who should be competing in races of varying distances up to 15 kilometers or 10 miles. This runner should try to race once or twice a month, but not weekly. When adding mileage, this runner should increase the long runs first, the hard days (Tuesday/Thursday) second and lastly, the easy days.

Month 2: Continue to increase mileage to 50+ miles a week. A typical week:

Monday	4 miles easy
Tuesday	10 miles moderate
Wednesday	4 miles easy

Thursday	3 miles easy, 4 miles hard, 3 miles moderate (total 10 miles)
Friday	5 miles easy
Saturday	5 miles moderate or including a few long, timed intervals, i.e., 1320s or miles, at four-mile race pace
Sunday	13 to 15 miles easy
Total:	51 to 53 miles

Month 3: Mileage should be up to 55 miles per week. Runner should try to find longer races (15 to 25 km.) or do sustained runs to prepare for marathon. May also want to race at shorter distances for variety and speed work. Increased fitness should bring improved times in shorter races. May want to add morning runs. A typical week:

	A.M.	P.M.
Monday		3 to 5 miles easy
Tuesday	2 miles	8 miles, including fartlek
Wednesday		3 to 5 miles easy
Thursday		2 miles easy, 4 miles at 10-mile race pace (i.e. if this runner had recently run a 10-miler in 7:00 per mile), 3 miles easy
Friday		5 miles easy
Saturday		6 miles easy
Sunday	15 to 18 miles easy	
Total:	51 to 58 miles	

Comments: As mentioned in Month 1, Saturday or Sunday may become Race Day. Depending on recovery, this runner may be able to race a short distance on Saturday and still go for a long run on Sunday. Otherwise, this runner may give up one long run a month in order to race hard on the weekend (Saturday or Sunday) and then recovery completely by Tuesday's hard workout.

Months 4,5,6 : Should be devoted to training for marathon. Build mileage up to 60 miles per week in month 4, 65 miles per week for months 5 and 6. Might try for one or two weeks of 70 miles per week in the period 3 to 5 weeks before the marathon. Runner will taper down to 50 or 55 miles the two weeks before the marathon and approximately 25 or 30 miles for the six days prior to the marathon itself.

This runner should try to race 30 kilometers or 20 miles if possible during this period, or at the very least, a half-marathon. The runner should also try to race over shorter distances as part of his training program, i.e., on a hard day, warm up by running easily for 1 or 2 miles, compete hard, but not all out, in a 3 to 6 mile road race and cool down by running easily for another 2 to 5 miles.

A typical week during this period:

	A.M.	P.M.
Monday		4 to 5 miles easy
Tuesday	3 miles	8 to 10 miles including 3-4 miles sustained
Wednesday		4 to 5 miles easy
Thursday	2 miles	10 to 11 miles moderate
Friday		4 to 5 miles easy
Saturday		1 mile easy, 3 miles light fartlek, 1 mile easy
Sunday	18 to 22 miles easy	
Total:	58-68 miles	

Comments: Racing, again, is an important part of the training. In some cases a long race (i.e., 25 km. and up) will substitute for a long run. While this runner may skip a long run occasionally in order to race effectively, he should be doing a minimum of a long run every other week in the three months prior to the marathon. This runner can expect to run somewhere between 3:10 and 3:20 for his first marathon.

It's very easy for the runner training for a marathon to get caught up in counting miles and setting rigid goals. Read your body. If you need an extra day of rest which means you'll only get 65 miles a week instead of 70, take that rest. Although you can't expect to feel fresh for every workout, be on the lookout for periods of staleness. Cut back for a week, give yourself some extra days of rest. Feel healthy and fresh before you plunge into your regular training regimen again. If you have given yourself enough time to train for something like a marathon, then you'll have enough time to allow yourself a day or a week within that program to allow for needed rest, due to injury, illness or general fatigue.

Runner #2: A 30-year-old male; 14 years of running background. Has run at national class levels at various times during his career. Trains very seriously for important road races. His goal is a 20 km. road race on July 4. He competed in several cross country races the previous autumn, ran a 2:21 marathon in early December, and then ran easily and enjoyably during his vacation period until the first of the year.

During January and February he does volume training to establish a strong aerobic base. In March and April he adds repetitions, fartlek and sustained runs, and is less concerned with mileage. During May and June he races extensively, primarily at shorter distances. His training during these two months emphasizes quality. There is considerable rest and only slight interest in weekly mileage.

Month 1: After just 40 miles per week during the holidays, he gradually works his mileage up to 75 miles per week by the end of the month of January, doing a light fartlek occasionally for enjoyment. This is his third week of training:

	A.M.	P.M.
Monday	3 miles	5 miles
Tuesday	3 miles	8 miles
Wednesday	3 miles	5 miles
Thursday	3 miles	8 miles with fartlek
Friday	3 miles	5 miles
Saturday	10 miles	
Sunday	14 miles	
Total:	70 miles	

Comments: His morning runs are covered at whatever pace is enjoyable. Afternoon and weekend runs are at a moderate tempo. As he gets fitter, these runs gradually increase in speed but stay at the same comfort level. He starts in January at 7:00 per mile and is running 6:30 pace by the first of February with the same degree of effort.

Month 2: Continuing to build mileage, this runner reaches 110 miles for the last week of February, with no emphasis on quality. Here is his biggest week:

	A.M.	P.M.
Monday	5 miles	8 miles
Tuesday	5 miles	13 miles (including 4 miles sustained)
Wednesday	5 miles	9 miles
Thursday	5 miles	14 miles
Friday	5 miles	8 miles
Saturday	12 miles	3 miles
Sunday	18 miles	
Total:	110 miles	

Comments: This is his most difficult week of the entire six months. He feels as though he is spending his whole day running. His easy days are not especially easy. On hard days he generally goes farther, not faster.

Month 3: Glad to get into more varied training and less mileage, the runner becomes more creative, gradually mixing several forms of faster running into his plan. He also races every three weeks or so to help gauge his fitness and to get the "feel" of competition again. By the third week of March he is doing the following:

	A.M.	P.M.
Monday	4 miles	6 miles
Tuesday	4 miles	2 miles easy, 7 miles hard, 1 mile easy, 8 x 110 fast and relaxed with 110 jog between, 1 mile easy
Wednesday	4 miles	5 miles
Thursday	4 miles	3 miles easy, 2 miles with fartlek, 2 miles easy, 2 miles with fartlek, 2 miles easy
Friday	4 miles	4 miles
Saturday	9 miles easy	
Sunday	18 miles moderate	
Total:	85 miles	

Comments: He races a 7-miler at 5:05 pace during the second week of March and does a hilly 10-mile at 5:16 pace on the first of April.

Month 4: The runner continues enjoyable hard-day workouts which are giving him a feeling of comfort at race pace or faster. The third week of April he does this:

	A.M.	P.M.
Monday	4 miles	7 miles moderate
Tuesday	4 miles	3 miles easy to a grassy park, 6 x 1 km. fast (untimed) with 1 km. jog between, 2 miles easy, 4 x 220 relaxed striding on grass with 220 jog between, 3 miles easy
Wednesday	4 miles	7 miles easy
Thursday	4 miles	10 miles moderate
Friday	2 miles	5 miles easy
Saturday	2 miles easy, run 25 km. road race, 2 miles easy	
Sunday	7 miles easy	
Total:	82 miles	

Comments: Since the race is important and is relatively long, he does only one major workout, then rests for the weekend. He still runs more than 80 miles, although most of it is quite easy. He does 5:12 pace for the 25 km.

Month 5: Because May and June are during the track season, he takes advantage of the excellent competition available at shorter distances on the track. The faster pace of the track races (1500 to 10,000 meters) makes 20 km. race tempo seem comfortable. Because he has done repetitions on the grass during the previous two months, he is ready to train intensely on the track (which he enjoys) during the last two months before the big race. The emphasis is on quality training, short racing, and rest. This is the third week of May:

	A.M.	P.M.
Monday	3 miles	6 miles moderate with 12 x 110 relaxed on grass

Tuesday	3miles	2 miles on grass. On track: 3 x 220 (34 seconds) with 220 jog, jog 440, 1 x 1½ miles at 72 sec. pace, jog 1320, 8 x 440 (67) with 220 jog between, jog 880, 1 x 1½ miles at 72 sec. pace, jog mile on grass, 6 x 110 fast and relaxed with 110 jog between, jog mile on grass
Wednesday	3 miles	5 miles with light fartlek on grass
Thursday	2 miles	2 miles easy on grass. On track: 5 x 110 striding with 110 jog, 3 x 880 (2:20) with 440 jog, 3 mile jog on grass, 3 x 880 (2:20) with 440 jog, 5 x 165 hard with 165 walk between, 2 miles easy
Friday	2 miles	2 miles easy
Saturday		2 miles easy, 6 x 110 striding, run 5,000 meter track race, 5 miles easy
Sunday	15 miles moderate	
Total:	74 miles	

Comments: He races 5,000 meters in 14:05 which is near his career best. His mileage is dropping. Easy days often include some fast, relaxed running.

Month 6: The runner's empasis is now completely on quality training sessions and preparatory races. Mileage continues to drop as rest increases.

Here is the third week of June:

	A.M.	P.M.
Monday	3 miles	3 miles moderate
Tuesday	2 miles	2 miles on grass, 8 x 110 striding on grass, 1 x mile (4:30), jog 2 miles on grass, 1 x mile (4:25), jog mile on grass, 3 x 330 (45) with 330 walk between, jog 2 miles
Wednesday	3 miles	3 miles moderate

Thursday	2 miles	2 miles on grass, 3 x 165 relaxed with 165 jog, 12 x 220 (33) with 27 second rest (start a 220 every minute) 2 mile jog, 2 miles of fartlek on grass, mile jog
Friday	2 miles	2 miles easy
Saturday		2 miles easy, 6 x 110 striding, run 3,000 meter track race, 6 x 110 striding, 3 miles easy
Sunday	17 miles moderate	

Total: 64 miles

Comments: This last month of training looks very much like that of a track runner peaking. The road runner feels that the fast running and racing he does in the last month of the plan will bring him to a competitive peak. He runs the 3,000 meter race in 8:15 which is his best. He continues to do a long weekend run, so he is unafraid of the 20 km. distance although he has not raced that long in two months. He realistically feels his comfort in fast training, his fitness over shorter distances, and his experience in racing on the road will carry him through the 20 km. road race at better than 5:00 pace.

Runner #3: A female runner in her mid 20s whose best mile is 5:25. She has run a 3:12 marathon and is planning to run in several road races during the summer, highlighted by a traditional 10 km. road race which attracts all the best runners in the city.

Two months before the 10 km. race she is relatively fit having raced every two or three weeks while doing 40 to 50 miles per week. She ran the 10 km. race last year in 40:30 and wants to go much faster this year. This is the race for which local racers try to peak.

In the two months leading up to the race she plans to increase her volume, but only slightly. Her main goal is to do more quality running. She likes track training but feels it is best to mix it with fast running on soft surfaces. When she is feeling especially fresh she likes to push hard during road workouts.

She plans to race every other weekend at distances up to 10 miles.

Here is the third week of her two month training plan:

	A.M.	P.M.
Monday	2 miles easy	7 miles on the road including 3 miles hard
Tuesday		5 miles easy
Wednesday	2 miles easy	1½ mile jog to grassy area, 35 minutes of fartlek, 1½ miles home
Thursday		4 miles moderate
Friday	2 miles easy	2 miles easy. On track: 3 x mile (6:00, 5:50, 5:44) with 10 minute walk and jog between, jog 2 miles
Saturday	10 miles easy	
Sunday	4 miles easy	

Total: 53 miles

Comments: Her hard days are quite demanding, so she runs very easily on her light days. She does not race this week. If she did race on Saturday, she would replace Friday's interval session with a light fartlek or light jog depending on the importance of the race.

The sixth week of her plan:

	A.M.	P.M.
Monday	2 miles easy	1½ miles easy. On track: 3 sets of 880 (2:45), 660 (2:00), 440 (77) with equal distance jog after each run and 10 minutes walk between sets. 5 x 110 fast on grass with 110 walk between. Mile easy
Tuesday		4 miles easy
Wednesday	2 miles easy	2½ miles to a grassy area, 3 x 1 km. (untimed) on the grass at a fast, relaxed tempo with 1 km. jog between, 2½ mile jog home
Thursday		4 miles easy

ALL ABOUT ROAD RACING

Friday	2 miles easy	3 miles easy on grass, 2 sets of 5 x 220 fast on grass with 220 walk between, 1½ miles easy after each set
Saturday	10 miles easy or moderate	
Sunday	4 miles easy	

Total: 54 miles

Comments: The Monday session is intense. Therefore, Wednesday's run is an attempt at quality but without mental stress. She finishes the week with some of her fastest running of the two-month plan on Friday. The pace of her weekend endurance run depends on how well she recovers.

Without a drastic increase in mileage, in this plan she does a variety of difficult workouts, gradually increasing in their intensity. She gives herself plenty of rest and avoids the temptation to time herself on every hard day. Her goal, a sub-forty-minute 10 km. effort, is well within reach.

After the big race, she expects to do one quality workout each week, with steady runs on the other days. She will be able to race well for several weeks on this "maintenance" training.

Runner #4: A 35-year-old male who started jogging three years ago for fitness. After a year he began doing fun runs and low-key races. He has been road racing seriously for a year, having done 3:09 easily in his first marathon and 2:55 in his second. His goal is a 2:45 marathon.

Because the marathon is so demanding on one's time and effort, he is willing to commit himself to no more than a three-month plan. In training for his second marathon he felt that being a marathoner was like having a second job. A three-month buildup is reasonable since he already does fifty miles a week for his normal road training. He definitely has adequate background.

The major emphasis of his training will be on mileage, both weekly mileage and the length of his weekend runs. He will also emphasize sustained runs.

Here is a typical week in the first month:

	A.M.	P.M.
Monday		8 miles moderate
Tuesday		12 miles moderate
Wednesday		6 miles easy
Thursday		5 miles moderate, 5 miles pushing, 1 mile easy
Friday		5 miles easy on the grass
Saturday	10 miles moderate	
Sunday	16 to 19 miles easy	
Total:	62 to 65 miles	

Comments: This month he is concerned with volume, with only slight emphasis on quality. He has to be at work at 7:00 a.m. Therefore, he cannot do a morning run, and doesn't feel he needs it. Getting started in the afternoon is difficult but he usually feels exhilarated after a few miles. This month he races a 10-miler and a four-mile fun run, the latter as a "speed workout" the day after a 16-mile Saturday run.

In the middle of the second month he does this:

	A.M.	P.M.
Monday		8 miles moderate
Tuesday		3 miles easy, 12 x 440 (78) with 220 jog between, 5 miles easy
Wednesday		5 miles easy on grass
Thursday		3 miles easy, 6 miles fast and relaxed, 2 miles easy
Friday		5 miles easy
Saturday	10 miles moderate	
Sunday	19 to 22 miles moderate	
Total:	70 to 73 miles	

Comments: During this month he increases his mileage, and his training is more extreme—there is more fast running, more easy running, and less moderate running. He races

ALL ABOUT ROAD RACING

seriously at 30 km. and does long runs on two other weekends. The remaining weekend he does an easy run and relaxes the rest of the day. He is fit enough that Thursday's "fast and relaxed" run is well under 6:00 pace. He has to concentrate in order to hold the pace, but it is more exhilarating than draining.

Here is his training week three weeks before the marathon: (He runs a 20 km. race the previous Saturday and takes a light jog on Sunday.)

	A.M.	P.M.
Monday		7 miles easy
Tuesday		10 miles at a fast, enjoyable tempo (63 to 64 minutes)
Wednesday		5 miles easy on grass
Thursday		2 miles easy, 6 x 880 (2:35) with 4:00 jog between, 2 miles easy
Friday		5 miles easy on grass
Saturday	10 miles moderate	
Sunday	21 to 24 miles moderate	

Total: 67 to 70 miles

Comments: His long runs have reached their maximum length. He will go only 17 to 18 miles the following weekend. The Tuesday 10-mile is difficult because it is at marathon pace, but is satisfying. He'll be able to breeze through 10 miles at this pace in the marathon although it is quite hard to do it in a workout. The track session gives him an added feeling of confidence since it is far faster than race pace. Because the light days are getting easier, he feels more rested for the quality training he is doing. Because he is rested, his hard day results are pleasing and his confidence is buoyed. He does a moderate carbohydrate loading routine and is ready for another major improvement in his marathon time.

Runner #5: A 16-year-old boy who has run on the track and cross country teams in high school for two years; he is excited about beginning to race on the roads between seasons. He has run a 4:45 mile and a 10:15 two-mile, but has never run farther than eight miles on the road in training. His goal is to train through the winter for a 7-mile road race on March 1st. He feels that training for a road race that is much longer than the high school two-mile will help him to sustain his training through the winter.

Month 1: Cross country season ended in mid-November and he only jogged every other day for the next two weeks. Since he did just 40 miles per week during cross country season, then rested two weeks, his first month's goal is to gradually build his mileage to 45 miles per week with only a little fast running.

He runs five days the first week, doing 5-6 miles steady runs. By the end of December he does this:

Monday	8 miles easy
Tuesday	4 miles easy
Wednesday	5 miles steady, 4 x 165 fast relaxed striding on track with 275 jog between, jog mile
Thursday	5 miles easy
Friday	7 miles moderate
Saturday	AM, 6 miles moderate. PM, 4 miles easy.
Sunday	4 miles easy
Total:	45 miles

Comments: After a month of gradually increasing volume he feels ready to do more mileage, but also wants to begin racing and doing more varied training.

Month 2: He does a two-mile fun run on the pavement the first weekend in January, but runs only 11:05, feeling sluggish and speedless. This is not unexpected since he is emphasizing volume, not quality. In January he continues to build his mileage to his ultimate goal, 55 miles per week. His hard days become harder and more varied. The third week in January he does the following:

Monday	3 miles moderate, 3 miles fartlek, 2 miles easy
Tuesday	5 miles moderate
Wednesday	8 miles moderate

Thursday	5 miles moderate
Friday	2 miles easy, 5 miles sustained, mile easy
Saturday	AM, 6 miles moderate. PM, 4 miles easy
Sunday	7 miles moderate

Comments: The boy does not do morning runs during the week because winter mornings are cold and dreary. School starts at 8 a.m. He races a five-mile road run in 29:50 at the end of January. He believes with pre-race rest and another month of training he can handle that pace for the seven-miler on March 1st.

Month 3: In the last month before the major race, he emphasizes the difference between hard and easy days. He asks more of himself, but gives himself more rest too. Mileage actually drops.

Here is the third week in February:

Monday	2 miles easy, 4 miles sustained, 3 miles moderate
Tuesday	2 miles easy, 8 x 110 striding with 110 jog between, mile easy
Wednesday	3 miles easy, 2 mile fartlek, 3 miles moderate
Thursday	3 miles easy
Friday	5 miles moderate, 2 miles hard on pavement in 10:55, mile easy
Saturday	4 miles easy
Sunday	10 miles moderate
Total:	46 miles

Comments: The boy has done an adequate preparation for a seven-mile road race under 6:00 pace. He built his aerobic base, added some race-oriented sessions and increased the quality of those sessions, being sure to give himself adequate rest.

Having a race goal helps him get through a winter's training. After the race he should jog easily a few days and then feel ready for a good track season due to the months of relatively high volume training he has done, almost all of which have been off the track.

Runner #6: A 50-year-old woman who has been a sports fan for years but has only recently begun jogging. She first got a physical exam and was found to be overweight and sadly out of shape. She then went to the Parks and Recreation Department, and signed up for "Beginning Jogging." She walked and jogged on the track with her friends or her radio for five months. She lost eight pounds but looks like she has lost much more. No longer self-conscious, she is ready to leave the track because it is boring. She generally does two miles non-stop, but has done three, and now wants to go further. Many of her younger friends run in races; she decides to enter some low-key ones. Her goal is to run a 10-kilometer race.

Our runner enjoys running immensely, even doing laps on the track, and is in no hurry to get to her 10-kilometer goal. A Bonne Bell 10-kilometer race will be held in a nearby town in four months. This is a reasonable goal for her.

To be able to run 10-kilometers comfortably and competively she must build her mileage from its current two miles five days a week to at least 25 miles a week. There should be no emphasis on running faster. She will probably speed up (with no greater feeling of effort) as she gets fitter.

Month 1: Continuing the five-day-a-week pattern because Saturday and Sunday are unavailable for running, she must very gradually increase her mileage. The simplest way is to add a mile to one run the first week, to two runs the second week, etc. The fourth week would look like this:

Monday	3 miles
Tuesday	3 miles
Wednesday	2 miles
Thursday	3 miles
Friday	3 miles
Saturday	rest
Sunday	rest
Total:	14 miles

Comments: She should be going off the track once or

twice a week. She can roughly time her three-mile runs on the track to get an idea how long to run when she is off the track. Runners usually develop favorite routes and come to dislike steady runs on the track.

Month 2: The next step should be a further increase in mileage, using the method as before. We suggest keeping the Wednesday run at two miles as a built-in easy day and also as a reminder that a two-mile run once was a maximal effort. The last week in month 2:

Monday	4 miles
Tuesday	4 miles
Wednesday	2 miles
Thursday	4 miles
Friday	4 miles
Saturday	rest
Sunday	rest
Total:	18 miles

Comments: By the end of month 2, she may feel no need to even go to the track to start the run. Running out the front door saves time.

Month 3: The pattern now should be clear. She should add another mile a week until the fourth week looks like this:

Monday	5 miles
Tuesday	5 miles
Wednesday	2 miles
Thursday	5 miles
Friday	5 miles
Saturday	rest
Sunday	rest
Total:	22 miles

Comments: By this stage of fitness she should be sure she can handle 10-kilometers the following month. She will probably have several five-mile routes and she will enjoy the variety of scenery. The two-mile run on Wednesday could easily have become a time trial which might be fun to do occasionally but is not recommended every Wednesday. She may wish to forego one weekday training run and do a 2-4 mile fun run instead, simply to get the feel of a "race" in which she will be compelled to run a little faster than usual.

Month 4: The pattern should vary in the final month, since the runner must show herself that she can handle the 10-kilometer distance comfortably. She should do a 6-mile run the first week and do two of them the second. The third week she should do a 7-mile run as well as a 6-miler. The fourth week she should do an 8-miler and a 6-miler. This break from the routine should not cause any hardship on the runner because of the program's gradual mileage increases. Here is the fourth week:

Monday	5 miles
Tuesday	8 miles
Wednesday	2 miles
Thursday	7 miles
Friday	5 miles
Saturday	rest
Sunday	Bonne Bell race
Total:	27 miles excluding the race

Comments: Early in the fourth month the runner should do another fun run as a learning experience. In the 10-kilometer race she should be sure to start off at her regular pace. Since her goal is simply to participate, she should try not to get caught up in the exuberance of undertrained novices. If she feels competitive, she can go harder over the last two miles, whetting her appetite for future competition.

4
RACING

As you plan a training program your goal is to prepare yourself to race successfully. But what is success? What is an appropriate goal?

Your training goal should be to train as intelligently and diligently as you can for a specific, important race. You should be able to stand at the starting line and say to yourself, "I trained hard and I trained wisely," or "I put together a training program specifically for this race and I followed it to the letter. I'm ready." After the race you should evaluate the plan and the race and decide if anything should be changed for the next major race.

Your racing goals should include some of the following:

1) To run your best time over a given course or distance.
2) To defeat other runners of similar ability.
3) To win the race, your division, or a prize.
4) To run intelligently and courageously.

This final goal is the most important. To be a truly successful racer you must train intelligently and intensely, then race intelligently and courageously. If you do these things, then the effort is a success. Beating someone or winning your division must be considered secondary. In truth you race against yourself. As 71-year-old marathoner, Mavis Lindgren said, "I'm not trying to go faster than another person, just faster than me." You try to be the best runner you can be. Your goal is one of self-actualization or self-fulfillment, a very subjective goal.

MEASURING SUCCESS

Some runners feel more comfortable with objective measurement. Time is the best measure because it eliminates other runners and allows you to compare yourself with past performances. The problems with time goals are obvious:

1) The course may be inaccurate.

2) The timer may misread the watch or, more likely, there may be a foul up in compilation of results that gives you an incorrect time. (The wrong time is usually faster.)

3) The weather may vary from race to race, speeding or slowing your run.

4) Courses that are of equal distance may be of unequal difficulty.

The best situation, of course, is to race over the same course repeatedly. A course may be inaccurate but at least it is the same length each time you run it although the weather may be quite different. Unfortunately, few courses are run more than once a year. Those which are run three or four times a year are usually not major races. They're handy for test efforts but are inherently of little consequence in a racing schedule. Thus, you're most often left to compare your fitness this year to your fitness last year in the same race. (There is a reasonable chance the weather will be similar, too.) Otherwise, your only alternative is to compare your times on several courses of varying difficulty and accuracy.

The track runner has an obvious advantage in the accuracy and similarity of the tracks he might run on.

Many runners come to be extraordinarily competitive. They measure success by whom they beat or how many people they beat. Most of us feel this way at least some of the time.

Beating people may be an obsession, a test of courage, an exciting challenge, or an interesting diversion. It's a rare runner who does not look through race results to see whom he's beaten and who's beaten him.

Racing can be a healthy experience. Some people call it a "microcosm of life." Others say you find out who you really are when you race someone. It can be a test of courage, but again it comes down to you against yourself more than you against another runner. If you run the race as intelligently and courageously as you can, you've won your race.

LEARNING FROM RACING

Every race can be a lesson. You may learn what you do well and what you do poorly. You may test a new racing strategy. You can check your breathing every mile to see how it changes. You can watch and later analyze other runners' strategies and tactics. You can note when you feel worst and when you feel best and try to discover why. You can continue to educate yourself to race and train intelligently.

RACING SEASONS

Races are so numerous these days that there are no seasons in road racing as there are for track and cross country. You make your own season.

Your first concern should be to decide what is important. If you race primarily for the thrill of racing (whether or not you consider yourself a fun runner), race as often as you want. When racing stops being fun, avoid racing for a few weeks.

Most people will want to emphasize certain races. You must decide what race or races you want to train for. You may pick up a series of short summer races with good prizes. None may be more important than any of the others. In this case you should train hard for the first one in the series, then train moderately between races. This program would be appropriate for racing weekly. Training hard and racing weekly is asking for trouble. You may be able to last six weeks training moderately and racing weekly before you feel a loss of form. It would be wise then to back off and rest at least briefly from both training and racing.

The more typical runner will pick a big race and direct his training at it. Typically, the race is a marathon, but it need not be. Let's say you are aiming at a prestigious 25 kilometer race. You should start planning for it as much as three months ahead of time. A month before the race you may want to do a 30 kilometer race to prove you can "go the distance" in a race. Some runners may find this unnecessary. You will certainly need to race three or four times at shorter distances. In this way you can gauge your fitness. Each race can help to make the slower pace of the big 25 kilometer race feel easier.

Most importantly, you learn to feel comfortable in races by racing. You don't want to overrace, however. Racing every week is too often, but running several races before the big one will help you cope with the psychological rigors of racing, simply because you've "been there before"—recently. Runners really do forget what it's like to race. Concentration seems to go most quickly.

Not all of the lead-up races need to be all-out efforts.

Again, decide if you want to run a race hard or if it is a weekend diversion or if it is something in between. Keep in mind, though, that these races are all part of the preparation for the big race.

You may find you are tired of training and racing after your three-month, planned effort. If so, take a rest. A complete rest is fine, although that means it will take longer to come back when your interest returns. Cutting your workouts back is a better idea. Consider yourself a fun runner for a month.

Some runners may find themselves motivated for more racing soon after the big one. This is where the fun comes in. If you cut your training back and race almost as often as you want, you may be able to maintain a peak for several weeks. You can probably get by on one hard workout each week that you race with easy runs on all other days. You would not be trying to get any fitter. You would be maintaining that which you had already worked to build.

You should realize that this state of fitness will start to go away in a few weeks. At that point it might be wise to be a fun runner again for a while before you launch another training and racing program.

MARATHON PLANNING

Most runners these days feel a compulsion to run at least one marathon. If a marathon were only 25 kilometers long, it would be a lot more enjoyable for those who feel obliged to run a marathon to prove they are "real" runners.

A marathon takes more commitment than shorter races. You need to alter your training and at least think about carbohydrate loading. And if you do really well or you really bomb, you cannot do another one two weeks later.

A minimum training mileage is 55 miles per week for eight or more weeks to run a successful marathon. A road racer should start lengthening his long runs as early as ten weeks in advance, and should gradually build up to at least 20 miles. It is also worthwhile to bash out a couple of runs that are 22 miles or more. Some experienced marathoners can handle 30 mile runs and they believe in them, but they don't do many of them.

As in all training programs, you are looking for specificity. In this case you're getting used to being out on the road a long, long time and being very stiff and tired. You've also got to get hardened to the common feeling in a long run that you simply don't want to keep running. This seems to be a loss of concentration related to glycogen depletion after many miles of running.

When you get right down to the last few days before the marathon, don't be afraid to rest. Three very easy days in a row leading up to the race may be just right. For any race, it's important to be fit and rested, not exhausted by trying to get fit.

WARMING UP/COOLING DOWN

If you plan to race as hard as you can, you should be ready to run race pace right from the start. Some people like to start out slowly and get warmed up in the first miles of a race, but the more serious racer will do his warming up before the race begins. You will develop your own warm-up routine which will include jogging one or two miles, stretching, a few easy strides and repeated trips to the bathroom. You should commence your warm-up period at least a half-hour before race time, allowing yourself at least five minutes of relaxation between the end of your warm-up and the beginning of the race.

You should also do some kind of jogging (or walking, if you're exhausted) after the race to help reduce muscular soreness the next day.

RACING STRATEGY AND TACTICS

Strategy in athletics is the "game plan." It is what you plan to do in a race. Tactics are specific changes in your strategy once the starting gun has fired.

Your strategy depends on your race goal and your fitness and who the other racers are. If you are only fit enough to try to make the distance, then you have no strategy because you have no opponent. Your plan should be to start slowly and keep a steady pace. In the late stages, if you're sure you can make the finish line, you can try to speed up to get a better time, but not at the risk of not finishing. It is far better to start slowly and finish fast than to start too fast, suffer a great deal and finish at a snail's pace.

If you are fit enough to make the distance, and you are interested purely in time, your goal should be to run even pace all the way. Predict your time, calculate even splits (write them on your arm if you must), and try to stay on pace. When you are sure you can finish, pick it up slightly, see how you feel, and decide if you can go even harder.

The fitter you are, the more sophisticated your plan can be. When you start racing against other people, you'll need a strategy or a variety of tactics to choose from, depending on what other runners do.

Remember that even pace is physiologically the most efficient way to run a road race. The less fit you are or the slower you are in absolute terms, the more likely you will need to use this plan. Major deviations from even pace will wipe out a slower runner more easily than a faster one.

The following list of strategies and tactics have been successfully used in important races by world class runners, either on the road, on the track, or over the country:

1) *Even pace as fast as possible:* If you are a pacer among kickers, this is often your best chance. You must set off at the fastest pace you can maintain, knowing that some runners with fast finishes or other strategies will follow as long as they can. You may lose the race, but even so you might get your best time. So might everyone else. They may or may not thank you for it.

2) *Burn 'em off, then slow down:* This is very bold and can be quite painful. You start off at a pace much faster than you can possibly hold the whole way. You must hope that no one can stay with you and that you will build a huge lead. Of course, you will have to slow down, but sometimes the others are so far apart and tired and disillusioned that they all "give up." Everyone runs in at the same speed, each runner looking

back, trying only to maintain his place. It is amazing to note how little changes in the second half of any race.

3) *Mid-race burst:* You may want to wait for the race to develop, for the pack to get comfortable with a particular pace, before you put in a do-or-die mid-race burst that is the same as "burning 'em off," except that you make your move when it seems most opportune.

4) *Long move to the finish:* This tactic involves following the leaders until a point where you are confident enough or scared enough that you take the lead and increase the tempo to one that you hope to maintain all the way to the finish. Some runners find themselves victims of those with fast finishing sprints. Some of the victims, though, are able to use a long driving finish which drops the big kickers one by one. Lasse Viren has been immensely successful with this tactic, being able to accelerate all the way to the finish.

5) *Surges to break contact:* Continually breaking your opponents' rhythm and concentration with surges of your own can be devastating. Each time your opponent must decide whether or not to go with you, and must hope you won't keep going. This tactic has been used by Vladimir Kuts, Ron Clarke, Frank Shorter and Henry Rono, among others. You obviously have to be very fit to use it.

6) *Pressure from behind:* Sometimes you can break an opponent by simply not letting him succeed with any aggressive tactic. If you are always there, following closely no matter what the leader tries, his confidence may wane. You may not even have to make a move to win the race. The leader may simply sag under your pressure. Or it may take only a small move of your own to break free.

7) *Wait and kick:* This is the classic fast finisher's strategy. Stay off the pace, move into contention, wait on the leader's shoulder and burst away in the last 100 or 200 meters to win. The time may be slow, but the win is often easy. You lose a lot of friends with this strategy, though, since you rarely help with the pace.

8) *Take the lead and slow down:* Your immediate objective is to slow the pace of the leaders to the pace you

want. An alternative goal might be to break up the rhythm of the other runners. Sometimes a big kicker, knowing he cannot hold a very fast pace, might try this tactic in order to be in contention late in the race. A weaker runner may try to slow the pace so he can hang with the group longer. A big name runner who is not very fit is most likely to try to slow the pace, hoping to still be in the hunt late in the race. This tactic is usually a last resort. If other runners are aware of what is happening, they should attack as soon as they see the pace slowing, knowing the runner who slows the pace purposely is probably defenseless in spite of his reputation.

9) *Draft as long as possible:* When you feel you are clearly outclassed, or are not up to par on a given day, hanging on to the group as long as you can is a viable strategy. In this case you never take the lead, but stay out of the wind, running in the back or middle of the group. You may surprise yourself at how long you can "draft" on this group. If and when you finally let them go, things get much more difficult. Suddenly you are running alone and your pace may drop off quickly. Often, though, you have a huge lead over the runners behind. Since very little happens in the last half of a race, you often can nurse that lead all the way to the finish.

10) *Catch 'em with even pace:* Sometimes you can outsmart a runner whom it seems you cannot outrun. If you are quite sure of what you can do on a given course, you can set off at your own pace and try to hold it all the way, letting your competitors go out as fast as they wish. You must have confidence that the way that is physiologically the best will work competitively. This method is especially useful in a marathon. At first you seem to be crawling along, eons behind your competitors. In the later stages of the race, though, many of them will "come back to you," shattered by their own over-enthusiasm, as you fly by at what seems to be an astonishingly fast pace.

This strategy calls for supreme confidence in your pace. It often requires great tenacity. As you tire in the later part of a race, it is easy to tuck in behind a runner you've just caught, saying to yourself, "I'll just rest a bit," rather than striking out boldly after the next runner.

Going out with the leaders requires only that you hold your place, but running even pace requires that you continually attack in order to move up to a high placing. At times that can be very difficult.

These strategies and tactics are most easily used by strong, fit runners. Most of us can attempt few of them. But perhaps most of us have never thought to try any of them or have never been in a position to try. Having an awareness of strategy and tactics can certainly increase the enjoyment of watching races (generally track and cross country) and such awareness may sometime prove useful in your future races as you become fitter and more experienced.

Many a victory and many a tussle back in the pack have been settled positively by the runner who simply had the courage to make some kind of a move and had the awareness to do it at the right time.

Some of the strategies and tactics mentioned above are calculated to make other runners go slower. You may or may not be in philosophical agreement with trying to force other runners to run more poorly. At the very highest levels of competition this is done. It is for you to decide if you should use such methods.

RACING FOR WOMEN, MASTERS AND MIDDLE-OF-THE-PACK RUNNERS

Among women and masters, only elite runners can avoid the crush of runners and joggers that is now common at most "t-shirt races." Those caught in the masses have the inevitable problem: no room to run.

If you are going to run a race which has a huge field of inexperienced runners who are seeded by expected time or pace, place yourself forward of the place you should be. There are enough novices who have an inflated idea or no idea at all of their abilities, that you will need to gamble a bit at the start to avoid the log jam.

When you do move up to a faster-paced starting group,

you should expect to flow with the crowd for perhaps as much as a mile before settling into your desired pace. Otherwise, like the novice, you become a moving roadblock for runners who started at their properly seeded position.

To figure your true pace in mass races, use your wrist watch to time how long it takes you to get to the starting line after the gun goes off. Subtract this time from your total time before you calculate your race pace.

If the race is really crowded and if mile splits are read aloud, calculate your pace from the mile point to the finish to get a truer estimate of your performance. It sometimes takes a mile or more of running for the pack to open up so that you can run your own tempo.

To cite an example, in the 1977 Boston marathon Jennifer Daniell of Redding, Ca., passed the starting line two minutes after the gun was fired. Because there was no room to run, she passed the mile mark in twelve minutes (ten minute pace for the first mile). Her final time was 3:16, but should have been about 3:11 since she would have run a little over seven minutes for the first mile on an unobstructed road. Her career best at that point was 3:14.

Crowded races are a serious problem for the middle-of-the-pack racer. Obviously, a runner can avoid the problem by avoiding mass races for serious efforts.

RACING AT ALTITUDE

The higher above 4000 feet elevation that you train or race, the slower your times will be. The higher you go, the fewer oxygen molecules there are. There isn't less oxygen in the air. There is simply less air. This means that for the same effort you will go slower at altitude than you do at sea level. At 4000 feet there is almost no effect. You probably would have to run intervals or a track race to notice anything. At 5000 feet you will notice a definite drop in your performance (about four percent worse in a one-hour run). Beyond 7000 feet world-class male marathoners have been hard-pressed to break 2:30 (about a six percent decrease in performance in a one-hour run, seven percent decrease in a marathon).

As a sea-level native, racing at altitude without any previous exposure at all, you are best off to race within 24 hours of your arrival. Several physiological adaptations begin to occur immediately but unfortunately things get worse before they start to get better. The first few days at altitude you reach a physiological low. Then your body's ability to produce extra red blood cells overcomes the short-lived negative adaptations and you begin to acclimatize in a positive way. It seems to take four to six days before you're actually better off physiologically than you were when you first arrived. You may be much better off, though, by having learned to cope with altitude during these few days. (Virtually complete acclimatization occurs in four to six weeks with diligent training.)

To race at altitude, whether on your first day or your 50th day, you must realize that the higher the elevation, the slower you will go. Going out too fast can destroy your race. Even pace is good and running the second half of your race faster than the first half may be even better.

You should plan to run a 10 kilometer race five to ten seconds slower per mile at 5000 feet than at sea-level, and 15 to 25 seconds slower per mile at 7000 feet than at sea-level. This will vary from person to person. All runners do not adapt equally to altitude. (You can expect significant improvement in your times after complete acclimatization, but you cannot expect to come close to your sea-level bests.)

When in doubt about what to do in a race at altitude, start off slowly and try to finish fast. You will probably find that most sea-level runners will underestimate altitude's effects. They will be sitting ducks late in the race if you keep your composure early and move up strongly in the second half of the race.

ALTITUDE TRAINING FOR SEA-LEVEL RACING

Some runners are sold on training at altitude to race at sea-level. Your red blood cell count increases at altitude. You learn to breathe greater volumes of air at altitude. Typically, you also hurt more at altitude in your training. Many runners delve deeper into their anaerobic reserves at altitude, learning to better tolerate lactic acid build-up.

Whatever the reason, altitude training does pay off when racing at sea-level.

The pitfall of training at altitude is that for the same effort you would run at sea-level, you will run slower at altitude. You may find yourself returning to sea-level feeling comfortable at altitude pace but having lost your comfort at sea-level pace which is much faster. Therefore you must try to do some of your altitude training at sea-level training/racing pace.

On the track you will have to run fewer repetitions or shorter distances or take longer rests. A sea-level workout of 10 x 440 in 75 seconds with 1:30 jog between them could be decreased to 6 x 440 or 10 x 330 or the rest could be increased to 2:30. However, running 10 x 440 in 80 seconds with 1:30 jog would be defeating your purpose. You would be running altitude training tempo to race at sea-level.

This same concept applies to steady-paced runs. You will run slower for the same amount of effort. Therefore some of your runs should be at the pace you will run at sea-level. You will tire sooner or be more uncomfortable through more of the run and will have to shorten the length of the run, but you will be "grooving" the pace you will need to run at sea-level.

When you begin training at altitude, do not try to increase your mileage or your quality of running. Your body will be under great stress. You may have headaches, nausea, diarrhea, or sleeplessness if you are at very high altitude. This is no time to be heroic and try to do more than usual. Remember, a great deal of your acclimatization occurs just by being there.

HEAT

Training and racing in the heat poses a serious challenge and a potential danger.

The dangers are heat exhaustion (which can make you ill) and heat stroke (which can kill you). Heat exhaustion is characterized by cold, clammy, whitish skin and a fast, weak pulse. Standard treatment is to cease activity, move to a cool, shaded place if possible, drink cool liquids in small doses, and lie down.

Heat stroke is characterized by hot, red, dry skin and no sweating, even on the hottest day. Standard treatment is to cool the body quickly by any external means possible: remove as much clothing as possible, pour water over the skin, rub ice cubes on the skin, even immerse the entire body in shallow water or an ice cube bath. The victim can take in liquids if he is able to.

Heat stroke is a life and death problem. It must be treated immediately.

Heat exhaustion, if not treated, can lead to heat stroke, so it must also be treated with great care and the victim must be under constant observation, preferably at a medical facility.

If you're in a race and you see a runner in either of these conditions, or a runner weaving, or a runner on the ground, stop and help.

Heat problems can occur on days that do not seem especially warm. Don't put yourself in a dangerous situation by racing all-out in the heat.

You will not get a good time on a hot day. On a cool day

ON HOT DAYS, WEAR
AS LITTLE AS POSSIBLE.

your heart pumps blood to and from the working muscles. The blood carries oxygen to the muscles and carries carbon dioxide and wastes from them. But on a hot day the blood must also be pumped from the core of your body to near the skin's surface in order to try to cool you. The heart has another job to do so it cannot do the first as well.

When you race on a hot day your body temperature rises, as it does when you have a fever. You hurt a lot more for the same pace, or you run slower for a more tolerable level of pain.

When you race in the heat, tone down your goal pace. This is an ideal chance to outsmart your opponent by realizing no one will be able to run as fast as on a cool day.

If you have any chance to drink during a heat race, drink! It's better to pour liquid inside you than to pour it on the outside. Water is just as good as drinks loaded with this and that. Replacing the electrolytes and glucose is far less important than replacing the liquid that you lose through sweating. Water actually is absorbed faster than most sports drinks.

You should be well-hydrated during the days preceding the race. (Your body weight should remain within two pounds of normal during hot weather. If your weight stays consistently low, drink more fluids to bring your weight up to normal.) On race day drink up to a pint of fluid ten minutes before you race and take in a half-pint at each aid station. Don't wait to start drinking until you get hot or thirsty. You must drink early in the race in order to utilize the fluid.

To acclimatize to the heat you need only train in it for two weeks. The most important thing that your body does during this period is conserve electrolytes (salt, magnesium, potassium, etc.) so that your sweat becomes more dilute.

If you must run an important race in the heat and don't have a chance to train in hot weather beforehand, you can run in extra sweat clothes for two weeks before the race. This creates your own personal, hot, humid climate. It seems to work well. Unfortunately, it also draws quite a few stares and is terribly uncomfortable.

When you race in hot weather, wear as little as possible. Men can run shirtless; women can wear halter tops or swimsuit tops. If you wear a singlet in hot weather make sure that it is loose-fitting, and preferably of cotton or some kind of mesh material. Don't tuck in your singlet; let it hang loosely, letting air circulate around your trunk. A hat or visor is also recommended on bright days when the sun is beating down. Run through every available sprinkler or hose station on the course.

After the race, be sure to get enough liquids to replace what you lost during the race. Commercial preparations such as ERG and Gatorade will help replace lost electrolytes and glucose as well. It is best to drink water first, however, since your primary objective is to replace lost body fluids.

COLD

Heat is much more likely to do a runner serious damage than is cold. Cold weather, though, can make you miserable and can keep many runners from training at all.

If you are forced to go to a cold climate to train or race, keep these factors in mind:

You burn only a few calories a minute at rest but you burn about 100 calories per mile as you run. Thus, when you step out the door in t-shirt and shorts feeling chilly in 50° weather, you may find that you are dressed just right after you get going. The same applies for colder weather. Remember the greater amount of body heat you will be expending. Avoid overdressing.

Also remember that wind is often the critical factor in how cold it really feels. A calm 10° F day can be glorious, but a 15 mph wind on a 10° F day can be torturous. This is a day to remember to run into the wind first, then run back with the wind. Doing the opposite is a mistake you should make only once. By running into the wind first you feel cool, but keep your clothing dry. Then you heat up coming home with the wind. Your clothes are wet with sweat when you arrive and you go indoors warm and sweaty.

If you start out running with the wind, you'll be sweaty when you reach the turnaround. And you'll suffer all the way home running into the cold wind in wet clothing.

Remember that layers of clothing can trap dead air between them to provide warmth. Layers can also be removed and tied around one's waist on training runs.

Wool is the only natural fabric that stays warm when it gets wet. A wool hat and wool mittens are great for cold or wet days. Ears and fingers are the first to need extra covering on cold days because of their exposed surface area. Mittens are better than gloves. Old socks on the hands are even better in races because you can throw them off and the loss won't be so great if you can't pick them up later or can't find them.

The tendency to overdress is common. It can be endured in training but is a significant problem in racing. In most cases it's better to err on the side of underdressing than overdressing. When in doubt, wear less.

RACING SHOES

Your main objectives in selecting racing wear are lightness and environmental control.

Like your running gear, shoes should be as lightweight as possible. In addition to providing protection from the cold or the heat or from wetness, shoes must protect you from hard running surfaces which may provoke injuries.

Your training shoes are characterized by a thick sole with an elevated heel. Your foremost concern in a training shoe is probably cushion. Racing shoes will have less in the way of reinforcements—stiff, leather-reinforced heel cups and toe areas. Their soles also may be less dense, causing the sole to wear out faster, but again be lighter. You should be able to wear the same pair of racing shoes in all kinds of weather and on virtually any kind of surface.

When you're in the market to buy a pair of racing shoes, you should first examine your needs. Are you prone to foot and leg injuries, especially Achilles tendinitis? You may opt for a shoe with cushioning more similar to your training shoes becuase your feet can't take the heavy pounding without a lot of cushion. Overweight runners or very large runners may need more cushioning than featherweight runners. Likewise, the runner who is a foot-pounder (rather than a floater) should consider more cushioning.

You also may have to choose a shoe with an elevated heel similar to your training shoe, because the stress put on your tendons by a shoe with a lower heel can aggravate Achilles tendinitis. A quick check of your training shoe will provide a comparison of the cushion under the heel of the foot and the cushion under the ball of the foot. On a pair of Nike LDVs, a training shoe, the thickness under the heel is 1.67 times the thickness under the ball. In the Nike Elite, a racing shoe, the thickness under the heel is only 1.33 times the thickness under the ball. Obviously, the lower is your heel in relation to the ball of your foot, the more stress your Achilles tendon will have to take in a race.

Fortunately, stretching regimens and the use of elevated heels on training shoes can reduce the problem of chronic Achilles tendinitis, allowing most individuals to wear the flatter, lighter racing shoes for at least occasional important races.

The sole material of a shoe should be light, but not so soft and porous that you can compress it easily by squeezing it. If you run virtually all of your races on hard roads, you can select almost any kind of sole pattern. A waffle or nub-like pattern gives good cushioning because the nubs can expand horizontally as they are compressed, thereby absorbing more shock. The greatest value of the nubs is in the traction they afford on slippery surfaces, notably mud, grass, wet roads and, to some extent, ice and snow. The nub-like sole is excellent for any kind of terrain and surface, even for track racing if you can't wear spikes.

Leather or nylon? Very few racing or training shoes are produced in leather anymore. Most manufacturers seem to favor the heavy-duty nylon or nylon-mesh uppers which are light but durable and breathe better than the old tightly woven nylon which had no absorbent backing. If you are considering leather shoes, remember that they take longer to break in, will stretch more and are harder to care for than washable, nylon shoes. At the same time leather shoes can give excellent overall support as well as protection from the wet and cold.

Just because a shoe is designed for racing doesn't mean that it need be so stripped down that it lacks the basics which make a shoe comfortable. There should be some kind of innersole in the shoe, and rough seams should not come in contact with your feet. The heel counter shouldn't be collapsible.

The shoe should flex at the ball of the foot, not under the arch. You're most likely to be running fast, and at times very fast, in your racing shoes, therefore you must be able to bend your foot for the important driving and take-off action which centers on the ball of the foot when you're running fast.

If you normally wear socks in training, wear socks when you race and of course, when you try on the racing shoes. Wearing socks is a personal decision but the added weight of the socks may be a fair trade for comfort (socks keep your feet warm when it's cold, and reduce heat build-up in the shoe when it's hot). Socks are also good hygienically because they can be washed after each using. The dirt and sweat absorbed by the socks is that much less dirt and sweat to eat away and smell up your shoes. Cotton socks are the most absorbent; wool is the warmest in cold and wet weather; nylon socks are hot in hot weather.

If you wear orthotics (foot supports) in training shoes, you may have some difficulty finding racing shoes to fit, especially if you have full-foot orthotics. Some racers are able to race without their orthotics but each case is individual. When in doubt, wear the orthotics and select shoes which will allow room for them.

Ideally, your racing shoes should feel springy and comfortable, like bedroom slippers, perfectly molded to your feet. Shop around for your shoes and query other runners about their preferences. Keep in mind that shoes are mass-produced but feet aren't. Even if you've been satisfied with a certain training shoe and want to replace it with the same, be sure to try on the new shoe and examine it carefully. Manufacturers have a habit of changing models. Even shoes from the same run can come out differently. You may find that the racing flat which was perfect for you the last time you purchased shoes is now too narrow for your foot, or too wide for your heel, or has a new sole which feels unstable. Be selective.

Break in your shoes before you race. Wear them several times for training runs. A race is no place to find out that your new shoes tear your feet apart, cause blisters, pinch your toes and rub your Achilles raw.

DRESSING TO RACE

Except for extreme weather conditions which were discussed earlier, your racing clothing should be simple and may not differ at all from your training clothing.

Wear your lightest, most comfortable clothing for races. The less clothing you can wear, the better. In most cases a singlet or t-shirt will suffice, along with nylon running shorts and whatever underwear you normally wear.

If you are in doubt about what to wear, dress in layers that can be removed easily during the race. Don't drag along extra clothing, such as rain-soaked sweatshirts, which are only excess baggage. You have, no doubt, seen plenty of examples of what not to wear in a race—i.e., full warm-up suits, cut-off sweat pants under boxer shorts, full-length levis, even the zoot suits and tuxedos of the Bay-to-Breakers crowd.

Avoid clothing that binds or chafes. You can reduce friction by applying vaseline to the offending area. Wear your racing outfit during training sessions occasionally, so that you will be confident during the race that your clothing is appropriate.

5
INJURIES

The best thing to do about injuries is to prevent them. In the training chapter of this book are several guidelines which emphasize moderate training. Overtraining is the surest way to incur a serious running injury. The training guidelines, if employed, will help prevent injury.

When you have an injury that makes running painful, one of the alternatives is to see your family doctor. The doctor often will suggest that you quit running. That's a great solution from his point of view. After all, if it only hurts when you run or because you run, then you simply quit running to eliminate the pain. Some doctors still don't understand the runner's compulsion for running. The doctor's simple, cheap solution to your problem is no better than a last resort for you.

Fortunately, there are other people to whom an injured runner can turn. Some doctors, particularly those who themselves run, are more enlightened than others. Athletic trainers affiliated with a club or school are usually of great help to those runners who have access to them. Orthopedists are medical specialists who deal with bone and joint problems. Podiatrists deal with problems of the feet and legs. It seems that podiatrists have shown greater interest in running injuries in general than have orthopedists. There are excellent "running doctors" in both fields.

Podiatrists interested in running injuries can be helpful especially with injuries caused by your running mechanics in combination with overuse.

Since each person is built slightly differently than everyone else, his running style is different than everyone else's. Some runners, like Frank Shorter, glide across the ground, their feet padding the pavement lightly. There is no jarring, no head bobbing, no lunging. Other runners aren't so efficient.

Neither the smooth runner nor the awkward runner will

EVERYONE HAS A UNIQUE RUNNING BUILD AND STYLE.

have many injuries if they each run a mile a day. They may have no injuries if they run 20 miles a week. But as they increase their efforts, it is likely that the awkward runner will sooner incur a running injury of some type, perhaps pain in the hip, knee, ankle or foot.

At its very simplest, use of a body tissue is fine but overuse leads to injury. For each person the point is different at which use becomes overuse. It seems that the smoother your running style, the more running you can do in a period of time without causing overuse and consequent injury.

Every runner will get hurt. Ideally, though, you learn something from every injury. You may ultimately know what for you is overuse. You may have a mental list of specific things to do to prevent injuries. An experienced, thoughtful runner may be able to do 75 miles a week for several months. But a few weeks at 90 miles a week may lead to injury in spite of all other precautions. This is caused by what for this runner is a combination of overuse and imperfect running mechanics. At 75 miles a week a slight variation from perfection may be tolerable, but at 90 miles a week the increased stress may lead to an overuse injury.

In addition to avoiding overtraining, you can do these things to help prevent injuries:

1) Maintain or improve your flexibility and muscular strength.

2) Keep your running shoes and street shoes in good repair by applying shoe glue of some type to the heel and other areas of the sole that wear down. Running in worn-out shoes will alter your running mechanics for the worse.

3) Maintain sound nutritional habits.

4) Get adequate sleep. Rest is just as important as training.

5) Deal with seemingly minor injuries early to prevent them from becoming or leading to major injuries.

Since an exhaustive list of running injuries would take hundreds of pages written by a medical expert, we list here the most common problems and how they are treated by athletes, trainers and/or doctors.

MUSCLE STRAINS OR "PULLS"

The most common muscle strain seems to occur in the hamstring muscles in the back of your thigh, but strains can occur in virtually any muscle if it is overworked. A simple muscle strain involves excessive stretching of muscle fibers. Severe strains involve a torn or ruptured muscle. A minor strain will feel painful and stiff when you move. Hamstring strains may be caused by excessive amounts of very fast running, combined with weakness of the muscle to start with. A trainer would recommend reduced activity, heating the muscle before running, icing it afterward, and mild stretching. Since muscle tissue does not regenerate, the scar tissue which forms must be stretched easily as it forms. The hamstrings are particularly vulnerable to strains since they are often weaker than they should be in runners. Strengthening the hamstrings by flexion exercises with weights can prevent strains. Muscle tears and ruptures involve swelling, discoloration, obvious weakness or significant impairment of daily movements like walking. They require medical attention and a professional rehabilitation program.

TENDINITIS

A tendon attaches a muscle to a bone. Tendinitis is an inflammation of the tendon which is accompanied by pain and sometimes a grating sound or feeling as it tries to slide back and forth normally in its protective sheath. Usually due to a mechanical imbalance and chronic or acute overuse, the tendon becomes sore and inflamed and may be sore to the touch. Typically, it will hurt when you start to run, then will feel better, then may feel weak or painful toward the end of the run. It will usually become stiff and sore after the run.

Tendinitis commonly strikes in the Achilles tendon which attaches the calf muscles to your heel bone. It also occurs around the ankle and in the knee area.

As with muscle strains, treatment usually involves heat before and icing after running. Sometimes anti-inflammatory drugs are prescribed by doctors. For Achilles tendinitis it also may be necessary to decrease mileage and speed, run on soft, flat surfaces, elevate the heels with shoe inserts, and keep shoe heels in good repair to keep your tendon in its proper alignment. Passive stretching of the calf muscles can help alleviate the strain placed on the Achilles tendon.

SHIN SPLINTS

Shin splints is a term that has come to be used for any pain on the front of the shin. In truth, it refers to the pain of muscle strains next to the inner edge of the shin bone. This problem, actually termed posterior tibial tendinitis or strain, is often caused by excessive flattening feet. The muscles next to the shin are attached to the bottom of the foot by tendons that run down from the muscle, behind the ankle bone and forward under the foot to the attachment. If the foot flattens too much or rolls to the inside too much in spite of having a high arch, great stress is placed on the tendons. This stress can be transmitted to the muscle which becomes strained.

Taping the place where it hurts probably will do no good at all, since you will be trying to treat the effect, not the cause. For minor pain, heat and ice may be sufficient (treating it like a typical muscle strain). One must be sure to eliminate the possibility of a stress fracture.

Increasing support for the foot may help a great deal. Runners have had success with shoes with higher arches, with taping up the arches, and with the mass-produced arch supports bought in a drugstore. You can buy surgical felt and make your own arch supports. Or you can see a doctor, probably a podiatrist, for a complete lower leg examination which may be quite expensive.

ANTERIOR COMPARTMENT SORENESS (ACS)

Anterior compartment soreness is often lumped under the "shin splints" heading. It is actually something quite different. ACS refer to pain in the soft tissue next to the outer edge of the shin bone. This is generally less serious than true shin splints. ACS is a swelling of the muscles which let your forefoot ease down to the ground after the heel touches. If you strike heel first, these muscles are contracted when the heel hits. They are holding the rest of the foot up as you try to avoid landing absolutely flat-footed. These muscles suffer a huge amount of jarring as the heel hits. Sometimes they swell up and hurt with every step. This is often a beginner's injury, but not always. Heating before and icing after are common treatments. Running on soft surfaces and temporarily reducing mileage will help a great deal. As a runner learns to run more softly (farther forward or more on the outer edge of the foot), less shock is transmitted to the shin muscles.

Better running shoes (those with more cushion) may also help.

ACS is rarely long-lasting, but if severe enough, the swelling can cut off the blood supply, killing tissue.

STRESS FRACTURES

A stress or fatigue fracture is a hairline break in a leg or foot bone. It is a classic case of overuse. Sometimes it is associated with unusual torque (twisting) of the legs due to one's mechanics. Stress fractures usually cause tenderness or pain at a specific spot on a bone ("point tenderness"). Unfortunately, treatment is normally an absolute minimum of two weeks complete rest. The lay-off may have to be eight weeks or longer. Stress fractures are particularly frustrating in that they generally cannot be seen on X-rays until they are healing (when new bone tissue is laid down).

CHONDROMALACIA

Chondromalacia is a grating pain under the kneecap. This is caused by the kneecap rubbing up and down slightly out of its normal alignment in the groove at the bottom of the thigh bone. Chondromalacia is often caused by torque of the shin bone when running. The torque is sometimes caused by a foot alignment problem, typically a weak, flattening arch or an extremely high arch which rolls to the inside.

Orthotic foot supports from a podiatrist or orthopedist may be the best bet for chondromalacia, although mild cases have been successfully treated by isometric and isotonic exercises to strengthen the quadriceps muscles which hold the kneecap in place.

PLANTAR FASCITIS

Many athletes unknowingly call plantar fascitis a stone bruise. The plantar fascia is a "rubber band" tissue, not a muscle, that attaches the bottom of your heel to the ball of your foot, helping give your foot its arched shape. Each time you put your weight down your foot flattens. When you take your weight off the foot, the fascia helps it spring back to its arched shape. Overuse, and perhaps poor support, can lead to an inflammation of the fascia, often at the rear end under the heel. It feels like a bruise, but it's not.

Supporting the arch while running (tape, home-made arch supports, mass-produced arch supports, orthotics) will often take enough stress off the fascia to let it recover. Icing after runs will help reduce swelling. A donut-shaped support around the actual point of pain also may help.

BLISTERS

Blisters are an overuse injury in a very acute sense. Most blisters can be drained after lancing with an alcohol-swabbed needle or blade. The entire blister should be cleaned with alcohol and covered.

Minor blisters can be lubricated with petroleum jelly and covered with a bandaid without being lanced first, in the hope that the bandaid will eliminate the rubbing on the blister so that the fluid inside it will be reabsorbed. If in doubt, though, it is better to lance it than to tape it and risk breaking the blister during a run.

When lancing (or relancing) a blister, open it at the lowest point to promote drainage. Never remove the outer layer of skin since it protects the soft skin beneath.

Do not lance blood blisters unless they are severely distended. In most cases you can treat blood blisters by covering them with vaseline or a petroleum-based lubricant and gauze.

CALLUSES

Calluses are areas of skin which harden and thicken to protect themselves from chronic rubbing by your shoes or socks. Switching or altering your shoe can prevent further buildup of the callus. You can have a shoe repairman cut a hole in your shoe at the point of irritation and then place a patch over the hole. Alternating shoes may help. Calluses can be filed or carefully pared down when they become uncomfortably large or thick. Remember, though, calluses are there to protect you. If a callus is very large, it is probably because of a significant problem which you should investigate. Small calluses can be filed with a pumice stone. Large ones are best pared down by a professional, but you can then maintain them with a pumice stone from then on.

STITCHES

A stitch, rather than an injury, is an abdominal pain that occurs when you run and usually ceases soon after you stop. Many theories have been offered about the probable causes of stitches. Two quite reasonable ones are these:

1) Pain under the rib cage may be caused by a diaphragm strain due to improper breathing. "Belly breathing" is the proper method of breathing. As you breath in, your lungs expand and your abdomen should protrude, allowing your diaphragm to lower, giving your lungs more room to expand.

Some runners raise the chest and suck in the abdomen upon inspiration. This prevents the diaphragm from dropping and apparently can eventually strain it, causing a stitch.

Runners can practice belly breathing in workouts. They might find themselves doing just the opposite of what's desired, particularly when they run fast.

When a stitch occurs in a race it is often worthwhile to stop and walk a few steps in order to relax, dropping the shoulders, slowing down the breathing rate, and establishing a belly breathing pattern. You can start off at a jog, then ease back into race tempo, and feel good again. You may give away a hundred meters but at least you'll be able to compete, rather than clutching your ribs for miles and hoping you'll finish.

2) The second feasible stitch theory involves pain in the abdomen caused by gas trapped in your intestines. Here again, stopping in a race may be useful when combined with leaning over and either massaging the area or forcing your fingers as deeply as possible into the area. This will help move the trapped gas along your intestine. As you start moving again it would be wise to make sure that you're belly breathing.

MATERIALS FOR TREATMENT OF INJURIES

Most injuries can be prevented. If caught early enough, they will cause minimal disruption of training. Some injuries can be self-treated. A good trainer or doctor can be of immeasurable aid in getting you back on the roads when you've overstressed and injured yourself.

When self-treating an injury, heat is best applied by a hot water bottle wrapped in a moist towel. This moist heat is more penetrating than dry heat like that produced by a heating pad. Treatment should last 10 to 15 minutes.

Icing of large areas should be done with an ice bag of some kind, preferably a relatively thick, reusable one. Smaller areas can be iced with an ice cup. It is easiest to buy styrofoam cups, fill them with water, place them in the freezer, and use them when needed. The cup can be partially peeled away, leaving exposed ice but also giving you protection for your hand as you rub the inflamed area. Icing can be done for 20 to 25 minutes.

6
AUXILIARY AIDS FOR RUNNERS

Specificity of training, as emphasized earlier, tells you that running is the best way to get in shape for running. There are no magic formulas of diet or exercises that will guarantee you the racer's edge, but certain aspects of your daily routine can influence your race performance.

Stretching, weight-lifting and nutrition all can play a role in your development as a road racer.

STRETCHING

Runners who don't stretch can be identified easily by their inability to touch their toes and by their general inflexibility. The repetitive pounding of running tends to shorten your muscles and make them inflexible. Slow, static stretching can help counteract that shortening of the muscles.

A conscientious program of stretching will give you the flexibility to have a wider range of movement when you run. A good road racer runs economically, with shorter strides than the track runner because he trains and races slower. Yet he has the capacity to lengthen his stride as he runs faster and to lift his knees and charge up hills. The road racer's stride should not be shortened needlessly and permanently due to tight and inflexible hamstrings.

Besides allowing you to enjoy a more fluid stride, stretching religiously greatly reduces your chance of injury. Your Achilles tendon, for example, can be easily strained when the calf muscles are not stretched, but are instead allowed to get "bunchy" from running. These shortened, unyielding calf muscles put excessive stress on the Achilles tendon. Daily stretching keeps the muscles long and supple, taking the stress off the tendon.

You should incorporate some kind of brief stretching routine into every workout or race warm-up and you should develop a more sophisticated stretching program to be done daily or at least five times a week, either after a regular workout or as a separate session, perhaps just before you go to bed, or when you get up (although most people are the least flexible when they first arise).

There are hundreds of stretching exercises; you may have your favorites already. Do the exercises which you like best, but be sure to work on the flexibility of these areas: hamstrings, quadriceps, calves, back, and shoulders.

Before you run, or as part of your warm-up program prior to a hard workout or race, stretch your hamstrings, quadriceps and calves. Simple wall-pushes and stand-and-reach exercises will suffice for the hamstrings and calves. To stretch your quadriceps, stand on one leg and bend your other knee, bringing your heel as close to your buttocks as possible, with your hand grasped around your ankle and your thigh nearly vertical. Remember to stretch slowly. Do not bounce. Do not lunge. After stretching slowly, release slowly. Add a few trunk twists and arm swings to loosen your upper body.

Your more sophisticated stretching program should take five or ten minutes, but don't hurry through it. Find a place where you can lie down comfortably—a carpet or mat does nicely, as does dry grass.

ALL ABOUT ROAD RACING

Your routine should include sit-and-reach exercises which stretch your hamstrings and back. Straddle leg sit-and-reach exercises will help stretch your groin and adductor muscles. The "plow" exercise—lie on your back and bring your legs over your head in an attempt to touch your toes to the floor with your legs straight—is particularly good for stretching your back and hamstrings. The reclining hurdler's position will stretch your quadriceps, as will the "kneeling mummy" which also strengthens your abdominals.

In a standing position, try to touch your fingers behind your back, one hand over your shoulder and one hand under. Change sides, and put the opposite hand over the shoulder. You will probably be more flexible on one side than the other.

This session also should include some simple calisthenics to help strengthen weak muscle areas. Abdominal exercises are important, especially for runners who tend to be sway-backed or who have lower back problems. Abdominals (modified curl-ups) are best. Lie down with bent legs, arms behind your head. Rise up just enough so that your shoulder blades leave the ground. You should be able to feel your abdominal muscles tighten. Return to the ground and repeat. Do not rise to a sitting position since doing so works the iliopsoas muscle which is already relatively too strong, contributing to sway-back. Your abdominal muscles are the ones which need strengthening because they must keep your pelvis under your hips, rather than tilted out behind.

Women, especially, should be encouraged to do push-ups—true push-ups. Developing a reasonable amount of upper body strength is a worthwhile goal for any woman runner. At the very least, a runner should be strong enough to run erectly with shoulders squared rather than rounded. Better runners should have the muscular strength and endurance to drive their arms powerfully through the relatively wide range of motion required for sprinting. Most women are so weak in their upper bodies that they can't do more than one or two push-ups. Rest several minutes, then do another. Repeat the process. In subsequent days you will be able to increase the number and shorten the rest. Try to work up to 25 push-ups, even if you have to do them in two or three sets, with a minute's rest between each set.

WEIGHT LIFTING

If you have the interest and the facilities, you may want to try a moderate program of weight-lifting. Women, more than men, need to build upper body strength. Whether you're working with free weights or a weight-machine (such as the Universal Gym), keep your weight program light. Emphasize repetitions, not weight. You'll probably find one or two circuits of bench press, seated shoulder press, latissimus pull and upright rowing to be sufficient if you have access to a weight-machine. You may want to alternate lifting and stretching on each circuit (for instance, bench press followed by sit and reach).

Running provides sufficient weight-lifting for your lower body, but you may want to do some specific lifting to correct certain mechanical problems in your running.

Some road racers have an imbalance in the strength ratio of their quadricep muscles to their hamstring muscles, resulting

SHOULDER (MILITARY) PRESS
As in all lifts, come to full extension. Work through a full range of motion. Do 8-15 repetitions at the heaviest possible weight. Keep your back straight; do not arch backward.

LATISSIMUS PULL

Kneeling on one or both knees, pull the bar down alternately in front and behind your head. Do 8-15 reps at the heaviest possible weight.

UPRIGHT ROWING

Standing as close to the machine as possible, keeping your back straight, using an overhead grip (hands close together), lift the bar to shoulder level, 8-15 times with the heaviest weight possible. Elbows are always above the bar.

BENCH PRESS

With shoulder directly under your wrists, push vertically to full extension 8-15 times at heaviest weight possible.

DOUBLE LEG EXTENSION

From a sitting position, lift with both legs. Come to full extension at the knee. Grasp bench with hands if needed. Do 10-20 reps at heaviest weight possible.

SINGLE LEG EXTENSION

Using one leg, follow procedure described for double leg extension. Do 10-20 reps. If your legs are equally strong, skip this lift. If one leg is weaker, do this lift with the weaker leg only.

SINGLE LEG FLEXION

Lying prone on the bench, do 10-20 repetitions with the heaviest weight possible. Lift until your lower leg (shin) is vertical. Most people can only lift 10-30 pounds. If one leg is weaker than the other, do an extra set of reps with the weaker leg after a brief rest. Double leg flexion is not recommended because it is easy to let the stronger leg do more of the.work.

in a too-short stride and an appearance of dragging one's legs while running. Other runners may have one leg that's stronger than another, causing slight stride discrepancies. You can test the strength of your legs on a weight-machine by sitting upright on the leg machine and doing knee extensions, first with the left leg and then the right, at gradually increasing weights. Find the heaviest weight at which you can do one complete lift (180° at knee). Do the same by lying face down on the leg machine and lifting increasing weights to a 90° flexion angle at your knee. You may find one leg is stronger than the other, which is undesirable. You may also find that your maximum lift in the prone, flexion position is less than sixty percent of your maximum in the seated, extension position. This means that your hamstrings are less than adequate in relation to your quadriceps. This causes the leg-dragging appearance in running.

You can strengthen the weaker muscles by working them more than the stronger muscles. Do a brief lifting routine for both sets of muscles, then do additional lifts on the weak muscles.

DIET

The road racer needs no secret diet formulas, except for good, sound nutrition.

Vegetarians and junk food eaters alike seem to find success at the highest levels. Who's to say that the junk food eater might do even better if he became a vegetarian, or vice versa?

As a racer, you have three basic diet concerns: a balanced diet, a high percentage of carbohydrates and light body weight.

Just like every other individual, you need healthy foods to help you sustain a healthy body. And that means a daily diet which includes the basic four food groups: 1) milk, 2) breads, cereals and starchy vegetables, 3) fruits and vegetables, and 4) meat, fish and poultry. Since you are a runner, you also need a constant supply of carbohydrates because carbohydrates fuel your muscles in running. Close to 65 percent of your diet should be carbohydrates, at least 15 percent proteins and less than 20 percent fats.

Due to the high caloric content of sugar-ladened

carbohydrate foods (as well as the lack of other nutritive substances in those foods), you're best off getting your carbohydrates through breads and cereals, starchy vegetables and fruits.

Your daily diet should include four servings of milk, two servings of meat, four servings of grain and four servings of fruits and vegetables.

You probably have noticed by now that the fittest racers are generally the leanest racers. If you are running 70 miles a week, you probably have no weight worries because your running burns up an extra 700 calories a day, meaning that you can consume something close to 2700 calories a day if you're a woman and 3200 calories a day if you're a man, and maintain your weight. If you are overweight, use the old tried and true method of counting calories. Keep track of what you eat and the calories you consume, and work hard to eliminate 500 calories a day from your normal diet. This may mean cutting out desserts, or taking smaller servings or eliminating snacks after dinner, but if you stick with it, you should lose one pound a week which adds up to a tidy sum of 10 pounds in 10 weeks of calorie watching.

Be selective in your eating habits. A brand-name or fast food calorie counter book will open your eyes. Finding out that a Big Mac has 556 calories, that one plain cake donut from Dunkin' Donuts has 240 calories or that a banana split from Dairy Queen has 580 calories may help you readjust your eating preferences.

CARBOHYDRATE LOADING

Carbohydrate loading is a potentially dangerous way to manipulate your diet the week before a long race. It can significantly improve your performance in any race longer than 90 minutes in duration.

The scientific basis of carbohydrate loading is this:

Your body prefers to burn glycogen rather than fat to produce energy during exercise. Glycogen is stored in limited amounts in your body while stores of fat in the body are virtually unlimited (for energy production purposes). Carbohydrates in your food become glycogen stored in your muscles and liver. When you run long enough to burn up all the glycogen, you must burn fat in order to keep going. But this fat metabolism will not let you run as fast for the same effort.

In the late stages of a very long race many runners slow down drastically—sometimes by several minutes per mile. One reason for this is the depletion of the body's glycogen reserves and the changeover to fat metabolism.

The carbohydrate loading diet lets you store more glycogen so you can go farther before converting to fat metabolism.

This is what a loading experiment would look like in a laboratory:

A runner is placed on a stationary bike. He pedals moderately with one leg only for an hour or more until he is exhausted. The muscles of both legs are checked for glycogen content and the exercised leg is found to have almost no glycogen stores while the other leg has normal values. After two or three days of rest and a high carbohydrate diet, the legs are checked again. The exercised leg has an abnormally high level of stored glycogen and the other leg still has only normal amounts.

Depleting the glycogen stores in one leg causes the body to produce excessive amounts of an enzyme which allows glycogen storage. When the body has access to unusually large amounts of carbohydrates, more than the normal amount of glycogen gets stored in the muscles of the exercised leg because of the presence of extra amounts of this glycogen-storing enzyme.

This scientific fact can be applied to a runner training for a long race—any race which takes significantly longer than 90 minutes (approximately the length of time that normal glycogen stores last during heavy exercise).

The loading diet, however, can work drastic changes on your body and should not be attempted by anyone with health problems. It is generally suggested that people over age 30 do a moderate version of loading before trying the most severe version. It also should be recognized that a runner in the middle of this diet spends several days in a generally weakened condition. He may therefore be unusually susceptible to illness and injury.

It is also recommended that the diet be used a maximum of three times a year.

THE SEVERE LOADING DIET

The severe loading diet is the standard carbohydrate loading regimen. It is most often written about. Unfortunately, it is the one that people try first, when actually it should be used only after trying a more moderate variation for an earlier race.

Here is the procedure to follow:

If the marathon (or other race) is on Sunday morning, go for a long run the previous Sunday. Eat a very low carbohydrate diet and drink plenty of water the rest of the day and every day through Wednesday. Try to train normally. You probably will not be able to.

Rather than listing what foods to eat and what foods to avoid, we suggest you buy or get from the library *The Brand Name Nutrition Counter* by Jean Carper or a similar book which lists the fat, protein and carbohydrate content of many foods.

Do not avoid carbohydrates completely. Fifty grams per day is required for body functions.

You may find that you can barely run after a few days of almost no carbohydrates. If so, we suggest you try the two-day depletion diet listed below the next time you choose to load. It is necessary to run, however, since it is the working muscles which must be depleted.

Theoretically, you should try a fairly rigorous run on Wednesday to be sure you have depleted as completely as possible.

Make a drastic switch in your food intake starting Thursday morning by adding carbohydrates to your diet. Continue to drink large amounts of water, since water is stored with glycogen. Cut back your training; run the minimum amount that you can handle psychologically. The fewer miles, the better.

Do not overeat. Eat normal meals but replace some fats and proteins with carbohydrates—for example, less salad and more potatoes, less meat and a slightly larger dessert. Have a pasta dish for dinner. This phase of the diet, however, is not a license to be a glutton. Use common sense.

You will gain weight. Most of the weight will be water which can be useful to help avoid dehydration and electrolyte imbalance during the race.

This is the most rigorous version of the loading diet. You may find yourself weak and dizzy during the depletion stage. You may have headaches or be unable to concentrate. This diet has been described as "self-induced flu." If you are feeling thoroughly rotten, a small amount of carbohydrate may make you feel better without destroying the effect.

THE MODERATE LOADING DIET

For those who have tried the full diet above and choose not to do it again, and for those who are experimenting with loading for the first time, the two-day depletion diet is advisable.

Follow this schedule:

Train and eat normally until the Tuesday morning before a Sunday marathon. Drastically reduce your carbohydrate intake all day Tuesday and Wednesday. Train normally during those two days. Increase the mileage or intensity slightly on your easy day if you wish. You will probably feel sluggish by Wednesday afternoon. Begin eating carbohydrates on Thursday morning (after a morning run if you normally take one or if you can squeeze in a morning workout before breakfast). The final three days of the diet should be the same as in the first method listed above.

An experienced runner tried this variation of the diet for the 1978 Nike Marathon. He started the depletion phase on Tuesday morning and ran a light fartlek over a hilly, five-mile loop that afternoon, feeling a little sluggish. He did the same workout Wednesday morning and felt much worse—hardly able to change speeds at all. Wednesday evening he did the same

**WILL A SPECIAL DIET HELP YOUR PERFORMANCE?
ONLY EXPERIMENTATION WILL TELL.**

hilly, five-mile fartlek again and felt slightly better but still listless. Thursday morning he tried the workout for the last time before starting on carbohydrates. He felt so weak that he could not finish the run, taking a shortcut home instead. After three days of loading he had a fine race in the marathon, running strongly over the last six miles.

THE INTRODUCTORY/SPECIAL SITUATION LOADING DIET

A final variation, the one-day depletion, may be useful for the first attempt at loading. It is the least severe of the three. It is also practical for someone who, for any reason, cannot deplete for several days.

Follow this method:

Train and eat normally until Wednesday morning. Eat

virtually no carbohydrates Wednesday. Drink plenty of water. Run a lot of miles that day—for instance, five miles in the morning and ten or twelve miles in the evening. (Some people have tried three moderate runs on Wednesday.) Don't go for a 15 to 20 mile run. Don't run your race on Wednesday. Just burn up a lot of calories with moderate and easy running. Thursday morning (after a morning run, if possible) start eating a larger-than-normal proportion of carbohydrates as described in the other variations. Continue to drink lots of water and run only minimally.

All three variations of the carbohydrate loading diet have proven their effectiveness both in the laboratory and on the road. Loading is worth experimenting with, but you must remember that it is a drastic blow to your body and your mind. If in doubt, it is best to be moderate. You only need to store enough extra glycogen to get to the finish line. If a moderate loading diet gets you there with no drastic slowdown in the last stages of the race, then there is no need to try a more severe loading diet with all its accompanying hardship.

PRE-RACE MEAL

Whether or not you're carbohydrate depleting and loading, you're wise to make your pre-race meal one that emphasizes carbohydrates because they digest most quickly. Protein digests much more slowly. Fats digest slowest of all.

Since most races are in the morning, your pre-race meal most likely is going to be dinner the night before. Eat an early dinner and don't go overboard stuffing yourself. Stick with a pasta meal, or pancakes, rather than steak, or other proteins, and drink plenty of liquids. The morning of the race you may want to eat a light breakfast. Some runners race well on empty stomachs, while others feel that they need a moderate-sized breakfast of carbohydrates three to four hours before the race (which may mean getting up in the middle of the night). Others prefer to snack on tea, coffee or juice and a piece of toast a few hours before race time.

Do some experimenting with your eating a few hours

before a race. Just because you're used to grabbing a piece of toast an hour before you go for your long Sunday run doesn't mean that you'll be able to do the same thing before an important early morning race when nerves are starting to play havoc with your digestive tract. Many races have been spoiled by cramps, pit stops, gas and upset stomachs.

If you consistently have any of the problems just mentioned, try either eating earlier or eliminating certain items from your pre-race diet. Milk and wheat products are two common culprits. Likewise, too much fruit may bring on diarrhea. Be scientific with your diet. Note what you eat and when, and how you feel in the race. Hopefully you'll hit upon the right combination of foods and hours before racetime in order to make you feel comfortable at the starting line.

IRON FOR WOMEN

Iron deficiency anemia is a common problem among women. And for the woman road racer, anemia can spell the difference between a brilliant racing season and a lackluster one. It can be the difference between running 7:00 miles in a marathon or 9:00 miles.

Many women are chronically anemic due to either poor diet or heavy menstrual loss which further depletes an already low supply of hemoglobin, the substance which carries oxygen. Women also have less hemoglobin than men to begin with, thereby reducing their ability to carry oxygen. An anemic woman carries even less oxygen, causing her to tire more quickly and in the case of road racing—run more slowly. Signs of anemia include pallor, fatigue and unexplained drops in athletic performance or a lack of progress in training effect. You, the woman runner, may not feel in the least bit ill but may find that you feel somewhat flat or stale when you run and that the feeling doesn't go away.

A quick trip to the doctor or a medical lab can identify anemia. Your doctor most likely will prescribe iron supplements for treatment.

To avoid becoming anemic in the first place, eat iron-rich foods, such as fish and meat, especially organ meats such as liver. Dry cereals and breads to which iron has been added are also recommended. Unfortunately, some foods with a high iron content, such as eggs, spinach and some other green vegetables, are not good sources of iron because the iron is not available for absorption. Iron supplements can be purchased without a prescription, but don't start popping the pills without checking the dosage. You will need at least the USDA minimum daily requirement of 18 to 30 milligrams a day and can safely take up to 200 milligrams a day. (You only absorb a small amount of iron taken orally.) Any higher dosage should be cleared with your doctor.

APPENDIX

KILOMETER / MILE EQUIVALENTS

1 kilometer	=	.62 miles
1.5 kilometers	=	.93 miles
2 kilometers	=	1.24 miles
3 kilometers	=	1.86 miles
5 kilometers	=	3.11 miles
10 kilometers	=	6.21 miles
15 kilometers	=	9.32 miles
20 kilometers	=	12.43 miles
30 kilometers	=	18.64 miles
50 kilometers	=	31.07 miles
100 kilometers	=	62.14 miles
Marathon = 42.195 kilometers = 26.22 miles		

EVENT DIFFERENTIALS

100 yards to 100 meters: Multiply your time by 1.09
 (11.0 for 100 yards = 11.99 for 100 meters)
220 yards to 200 meters: Multiply by .994
 (25.0 for 220 yards = 24.85 for 200 meters)
440 yards to 400 meters: Multiply by .994
 (60.0 for 440 yards = 59.64 for 400 meters)
880 yards to 800 meters: Multiply by .994
 (2:25.0 for 880 yards = 2:24.2 for 800 meters)
Mile to 1500 meters: Multiply by .926
 (5:00.0 for the mile = 4:37.8 for 1500 meters)
3 miles to 5,000 meters: Multiply by 1.036
 (18:00.0 for 3 miles = 18:38.9 for 5,000 meters)
6 miles to 10,000 meters: Multiply by 1.036
 (36:00.0 for 6 miles = 37:17.8 for 10,000 meters)

Note: To convert from metric events to times for English events, divide by the appropriate number.

MARATHON PACING CHART

2:00 = 4:34.61	2:30 = 5:43.26	3:00 = 6:51.91	3:30 = 8:00.57	4:00 = 9:09.24
2:01 = 4:36.90	2:31 = 5:45.55	3:01 = 6:54.20	3:31 = 8:02.86	4:01 = 9:11.53
2:02 = 4:39.18	2:32 = 5:47.84	3:02 = 6:56.49	3:32 = 8:05.15	4:02 = 9:13.82
2:03 = 4:41.47	2:33 = 5:50.13	3:03 = 6:58.78	3:33 = 8:07.44	4:03 = 9:16.11
2:04 = 4:43.76	2:34 = 5:52.41	3:04 = 7:01.07	3:34 = 8:09.73	4:04 = 9:18.40
2:05 = 4:46.05	2:35 = 5:54.70	3:05 = 7:03.36	3:35 = 8:12.02	4:05 = 9:20.69
2:06 = 4:48.34	2:36 = 5:56.99	3:06 = 7:05.64	3:36 = 8:14.31	4:06 = 9:22.98
2:07 = 4:50.63	2:37 = 5:59.28	3:07 = 7:07.93	3:37 = 8:16.60	4:07 = 9:25.27
2:08 = 4:52.92	2:38 = 6:01.57	3:08 = 7:10.22	3:38 = 8:18.89	4:08 = 9:27.56
2:09 = 4:55.20	2:39 = 6:03.86	3:09 = 7:12.51	3:39 = 8:21.18	4:09 = 9:29.85
2:10 = 4:57.49	2:40 = 6:06.15	3:10 = 7:14.80	3:40 = 8:23.46	4:10 = 9:32.13
2:11 = 4:59.78	2:41 = 6:08.43	3:11 = 7:17.09	3:41 = 8:25.75	4:11 = 9:34.42
2:12 = 5:02.07	2:42 = 6:10.72	3:12 = 7:19.38	3:42 = 8:28.04	4:12 = 9:36.71
2:13 = 5:04.36	2:43 = 6:13.01	3:13 = 7:21.67	3:43 = 8:30.33	4:13 = 9:39.00
2:14 = 5:06.65	2:44 = 6:15.30	3:14 = 7:23.96	3:44 = 8:32.62	4:14 = 9:41.29
2:15 = 5:08.93	2:45 = 6:17.59	3:15 = 7:26.25	3:45 = 8:34.91	4:15 = 9:43.58
2:16 = 5:11.22	2:46 = 6:19.88	3:16 = 7:28.54	3:46 = 8:37.20	4:16 = 9:45.87
2:17 = 5:13.51	2:47 = 6:22.16	3:17 = 7:30.83	3:47 = 8:39.59	4:17 = 9:48.16
2:18 = 5:15.80	2:48 = 6:24.45	3:18 = 7:33.12	3:48 = 8:41.88	4:18 = 9:50.45
2:19 = 5:18.09	2:49 = 6:26.74	3:19 = 7:35.41	3:49 = 8:44.17	4:19 = 9:52.74
2:20 = 5:20.38	2:50 = 6:29.03	3:20 = 7:37.68	3:50 = 8:46.35	4:20 = 9:55.02
2:21 = 5:22.66	2:51 = 6:31.32	3:21 = 7:39.97	3:51 = 8:48.64	4:21 = 9:57.31
2:22 = 5:24.95	2:52 = 6:33.61	3:22 = 7:42.26	3:52 = 8:50.93	4:22 = 9:59.60
2:23 = 5:27.24	2:53 = 6:35.89	3:23 = 7:44.55	3:53 = 8:53.22	4:23 = 10:01.89
2:24 = 5:29.53	2:54 = 6:38.18	3:24 = 7:46.84	3:54 = 8:55.51	4:24 = 10:04.18
2:25 = 5:31.82	2:55 = 6:40.47	3:25 = 7:49.13	3:55 = 8:57.80	4:25 = 10:06.47
2:26 = 5:34.11	2:56 = 6:42.76	3:26 = 7:51.42	3:56 = 9:00.09	4:26 = 10:08.76
2:27 = 5:36.40	2:57 = 6:45.05	3:27 = 7:53.71	3:57 = 9:02.38	4:27 = 10:11.05
2:28 = 5:38.68	2:58 6:47.34	3:28 = 7:56.00	3:58 = 9:04.67	4:28 = 10:13.34
2:29 = 5:40.97	2:59 = 6:49.63	3:29 = 7:58.29	3:59 = 9:06.96	4:29 = 10:15.63

The figure on the left is a marathon time; the figure on the right is the pace per mile for that time. A three-hour marathon pace is approximately 6:52 per mile.

1-6 MILE PACING CHART

440	Mile	2 Miles	3 Miles	4 Miles	5 Miles	6 Miles
1:00	4:00					
1:01	4:04					
1:02	4:08	8:16				
1:03	4:12	8:24				
1:04	4:16	8:32	12:48	17:04		
1:05	4:20	8:40	13:00	17:20		
1:06	4:24	8:48	13:12	17:36	22:00	26:24
1:07	4:28	8:56	13:24	17:52	22:20	26:48
1:08	4:32	9:04	13:36	18:08	22:40	27:12
1:09	4:36	9:12	13:48	18:24	23:00	27:36
1:10	4:40	9:20	14:00	18:40	23:20	28:00
1:11	4:44	9:28	14:12	18:56	23:40	28:24
1:12	4:48	9:36	14:24	19:12	24:00	28:48
1:13	4:52	9:44	14:36	19:28	24:20	29:12
1:14	4:56	9:52	14:48	19:44	24:40	29:36
1:15	5:00	10:00	15:00	20:00	25:00	30:00
1:16	5:04	10:08	15:12	20:16	25:20	30:24
1:17	5:08	10:16	15:24	20:32	25:40	30:48
1:18	5:12	10:24	15:36	20:48	26:00	31:12
1:19	5:16	10:32	15:48	21:04	26:20	31:36
1:20	5:20	10:40	16:00	21:20	26:40	32:00
1:21	5:24	10:48	16:12	21:36	27:00	32:24
1:22	5:28	10:56	16:24	21:52	27:20	32:48
1:23	5:32	11:04	16:36	22:08	27:40	33:12
1:24	5:36	11:12	16:48	22:24	28:00	33:36
1:25	5:40	11:20	17:00	22:40	28:20	34:00
1:26	5:44	11:28	17:12	22:56	28:40	34:24
1:27	5:48	11:36	17:24	23:12	29:00	34:48
1:28	5:52	11:44	17:36	23:28	29:20	35:12
1:29	5:56	11:52	17:48	23:44	29:40	35:36
1:30	6:00	12:00	18:00	24:00	30:00	36:00
1:31	6:04	12:08	18:12	24:16	30:20	36:24
1:32	6:08	12:16	18:24	24:32	30:40	36:48
1:33	6:12	12:24	18:36	24:48	31:00	37:12
1:34	6:16	12:32	18:48	25:04	31:20	37:36
1:35	6:20	12:40	19:00	25:20	31:40	38:00
1:36	6:24	12:48	19:12	25:36	32:00	38:24
1:37	6:28	12:56	19:24	25:52	32:20	38:48
1:38	6:32	13:04	19:36	26:08	32:40	39:12
1:39	6:36	13:12	19:48	26:24	33:00	39:35
1:40	6:40	13:20	20:00	26:40	33:20	40:00
1:41	6:44	13:28	29:12	26:56	33:40	40:24
1:42	6:48	13:36	20:24	27:12	34:00	40:48
1:43	6:52	13:44	20:36	27:28	34:20	41:12
1:44	6:56	13:52	20:48	27:44	34:40	41:36
1:45	7:00	14:00	21:00	28:00	35:00	42:00

5-50 MILE PACING CHART

Mile	5 Miles	10 Miles	15 Miles	20 Miles	Marathon	50 Miles
4:50	24:10	48:20	1:12:30	1:36:40	2:07:44	
5:00	25:00	50:00	1:15:00	1:40:00	2:11:06	
5:10	25:50	51:40	1:17:30	1:43:20	2:15:28	
5:20	26:40	53:20	1:20:00	1:46:50	2:19:50	
5:30	27:30	55:00	1:22:30	1:50:00	2:24:12	
5:40	28:20	56:40	1:25:00	1:53:20	2:28:34	
5:50	29:10	58:20	1:27:30	1:56:40	2:32:56	
6:00	30:00	1:00:00	1:30:00	2:00:00	2:37:19	5:00:00
6:10	30:50	1:01:40	1:32:30	2:03:20	2:41:41	5:08:20
6:20	31:40	1:03:20	1:35:00	2:06:40	2:46:03	5:16:40
6:30	32:30	1:05:00	1:37:30	2:10:00	2:50:25	5:25:00
6:40	33:20	1:06:40	1:40:00	2:13:20	2:54:47	5:33:20
6:50	34:10	1:08:20	1:42:30	2:16:40	2:59:09	5:41:40
7:00	35:00	1:10:00	1:45:00	2:20:00	3:03:33	5:50:00
7:10	35:00	1:11:40	1:47:30	2:23:20	3:07:55	5:58:20
7:20	36:40	1:13:20	1:50:00	2:26:40	3:12:17	6:06:40
7:30	37:30	1:15:00	1:52:30	2:30:00	3:16:39	6:15:00
7:40	38:20	1:16:40	1:55:00	2:33:20	3:21:01	6:23:20
7:50	39:10	1:18:20	1:57:30	2:36:40	3:25:23	6:31:40
8:00	40:00	1:20:00	2:00:00	2:40:00	3:29:45	6:40:00
8:10	40:50	1:21:40	2:02:30	2:43:20	3:34:07	6:48:20
8:20	41:40	1:23:20	2:05:00	2:46:40	3:38:29	6:56:40
8:30	42:30	1:25:00	2:07:30	2:50:00	3:42:51	7:05:00
8:40	43:20	1:26:40	2:10:00	2:53:20	3:47:13	7:13:20
8:50	44:10	1:28:20	2:12:30	2:56:40	3:51:35	7:21:40
9:00	45:00	1:30:00	2:15:00	3:00:00	3:56:00	7:30:00
9:10	45:50	1:31:40	2:17:30	3:03:20	4:00:22	7:38:20
9:20	46:40	1:33:20	2:20:00	3:06:40	4:04:44	7:46:40
9:30	47:30	1:35:00	2:22:30	3:10:00	4:09:06	7:55:00
9:40	48:20	1:36:40	2:5:00	3:13:20	4:13:28	8:03:20
9:50	49:10	1:38:20	2:27:30	3:16:40	4:17:50	8:11:40
10:00	50:00	1:40:00	2:30:00	3:20:00	4:22:13	8:20:00

MILE/KILOMETER TIME COMPARISONS

Mile	Kilometer	Mile	Kilometer
4:00	2:29.16	7:00	4:21.03
4:10	2:35.37	7:10	4:27.24
4:20	2:41.59	7:20	4:33.46
4:30	2:47.80	7:30	4:39.67
4:40	2:54.02	7:40	4:45.89
4:50	3:00.23	7:50	4:52.10
5:00	3:06.45	8:00	4:58.32
5:10	3:12.66	8:10	5:04.53
5:20	3:18.88	8:20	5:10.75
5:30	3:25.09	8:30	5:16.96
5:40	3:31.31	8:40	5:23.18
5:50	3:37.52	8:50	5:29.39
6:00	3:43.74	9:00	5:35.61
6:10	3:49.95	9:10	5:41.82
6:20	3:56.17	9:20	5:48.04
6:30	4:02.38	9:30	5:54.25
6:40	4:08.60	9:40	6:00.47
6:50	4:14.81	9:50	6:06.68

ONE-HOUR RUN PACING CHART

Distance	Per Mile	Distance	Per Mile
6 miles	10:00.00	8 miles	7:30.00
6¼ miles	9:36.00	8¼ miles	7:16.32
6½ miles	9:13.32	8½ miles	7:03.44
6¾ miles	8:53.28	8¾ miles	6:51.42
7 miles	8:35.46	9 miles	6:40.00
7¼ miles	8:16.50	9¼ miles	6:29.16
7½ miles	8:00.00	9½ miles	6:19.02
7¾ miles	7:44.50	9¾ miles	6:09.24

Distance	Per Mile	Distance	Per Mile
10 miles	6:00.00	12 miles	5:00.00
10¼ miles	5:51.24	12¼ miles	4:53.88
10½ miles	5:42.84	12½ miles	4:48.00
10¾ miles	5:34.80	12¾ miles	4:42.36
11 miles	5:27.24	13 miles	4:36.90
11¼ miles	5:20.00		
11½ miles	5:13.08		
11¾ miles	5:06.20		

Other books from TAFNEWS Press...

LONG SLOW DISTANCE: The Humane Way to Train. Joe Henderson's alternative to backbreaking interval training for distance runners. (BRT-24) $2.50

CORBITT: The Story of Ted Corbitt, Long Distance Runner. The biography of the father of U.S. ultra-distance racing, crafted by John Chodes. Corbitt has run in more marathons than anyone else ever—almost 200 of them—and he's finished them all! 154pp. Illustrated. (BBT-1) $4.00

LYDIARD'S RUNNING TRAINING SCHEDULES. Second ed. 1970. Revised tables & schedules, 880-marathon. (BRT-25) $2.00

HOW THEY TRAIN, 2nd ed. In 3 volumes. **Vol. I: Middle Distances** (Wottle, Keino, 57 others). Paperbound, (BRT-15) $3.50; Hard cover, (BRT-16) $5.00. **Vol. II: Long Distances** (Shorter, Puttemans, Prefontaine, 57 more). Paperbound, (BRT-17) $3.50; Hard cover, (BRT-18) $5.00 **Vol. III: Sprinting and Hurdling** (Borzov, John Smith, Lee Calhoun, etc.). Paperbound, (BRT-19) $3.50.

GUIDE TO TRACK AND FIELD INJURIES, Arnd Kruger & Helmut Oberdieck. Concise, practical guide for the coach and athlete to the treatment and of common injuries. 96pp. (BPT-23) $4.50

HOW HIGH SCHOOL RUNNERS TRAIN, ed. by Greg Brock. Covers training programs of current and recent major prep runners 440-up, including Eric Hulst, Ralph Serna, Ronnie Harris, Rich Kimball, Terry Williams, Dale Scott, and about 60 others. (BRT-13) $3.50

COMPUTERIZED RUNNING TRAINING PROGRAMS, Gardner & Purdy. Thousands of computer-generated workouts take the guesswork out of training. Geared to the individual of every ability, every distance. (BRT-7) $6.95

PRE! A handsomely-produced book on the running career of Steve Prefontaine, who before his untimely death, came to hold every American record from 2000 to 10,000m. With many excellent photographs. (BBT-6) $4.50

TRACK AND FIELD OMNIBOOK. 2nd Edition, revised and updated 1976. Ken Doherty's colossal work, the synthesis of 50 years of competing and coaching in the sport. Many new excellent sequence illustrations. 525pp. (BAT-10) $13.95

TEEN-AGE DISTANCE RUNNING, Kim Valentine. Year-round program for developing the young distance runner. First readily available guide to coaching the teenage runner. 64pp. (BRT-34) $2.50

GETTING STARTED IN TRACK AND FIELD. This is the best thing we've seen for coaching of youngsters, boys and girls, in the various t&f events. 128pp. (BAT-3) $4.00

COMPETITIVE RACE WALKING, Ron Laird. Legal techniques, how to train, mental preparation, exercises, etc. Great sequence photos. (BRT-2) $4.50

TRACK AND FIELD DYNAMICS, Tom Ecker. Introduction to the dynamics of body movement in track and field events. Second ed. (BAT-9) $4.50

TRACK AND FIELD: TECHNIQUE THROUGH DYNAMICS, Tom Ecker. This new work follows up Ecker's *Track and Field Dynamics,* applying principles of the physics of body movement to each event in track and field. Profusely illustrated. (BAT-13) $4.95

Order from: *Track & Field News,* Box 296, Los Altos, CA 94022. Add 75¢ per book for postage & handling. Calif. residents add 6% sales tax.